Sept. 2010

Cady

Happy Birthday
to a Kindergarten
Mankato to Twin
Cities + freend.
Have a wonderful
year and may we
continue to share
fun times from
movies to grand
children.

Love,
Annie

A POCKET GUIDE TO
HERBS

A POCKET GUIDE TO

HERBS

Jenny Linford

Bath New York Singapore Hong Kong Cologne Delhi Melbourne

This edition published by
Parragon in 2010

Parragon Books Ltd
Queen Street House
4 Queen Street
Bath, BA1 1HE, UK

Produced by Atlantic Publishing

ISBN 978-1-4075-9542-9
Printed in China

Herbs are natural substances that
are used in medicine and must
always be treated with respect. This
book is intended as a source of
information; it is not intended to be
used as a medical textbook. If you
are undergoing medical treatment
do not take herbal remedies without
first consulting your doctor. It is
advised that any long-term herbal
treatment should be administered
under the guidance of a medicinal
herbalist. However, the use of a
herb for any purpose is at the
reader's own risk and the publisher
cannot be held responsible for any
adverse rections that may result
from the use of a herb, or its
derivative, contained in this book.

CONTENTS

INTRODUCTION

What is a Herb?

Throughout history mankind has benefited from plants in many different ways: fundamentally for food and shelter, yet also for several other purposes, including medicine, perfume, and cosmetics. Among these valuable plants is one group with a long history of use which we know as herbs. When one asks the question what is a herb, one begins to realize how wide any definition must be. Botanists use the term to refer to a plant with a stem that is not woody, yet the word has taken on a larger meaning. A keen cook would probably first think of a herb being a plant employed to add flavor in cooking, such as bay leaves, basil, or thyme. On the other hand, some people might consider herbs to be plants that are drawn on medicinally, such as echinacea or aloe vera. Mankind, however, has used herbs in many other diverse and ingenious ways: as insect repellents, for strewing on floors and scenting linen, for cosmetics and perfumery, for washing, preserving, and in embalming. This book, therefore, defines herbs as being plants with a history of use, whether that be as a flavoring or food (though the major food plants are not covered in this book), an aid to health, for perfume and cosmetics or yet other purposes. Herbs are often plants that are seen as health-giving or beneficial. Interestingly, many herbs have a number of historical functions. A plant such as thyme, which today we generally think of as a culinary herb, was used in embalming by the Ancient Egyptians and in herbal medicine as an antiseptic gargle. Sage, today primarily a flavoring, was thought to offer protection against snake bites, and used as a hair tonic and for whitening teeth.

Herbs range in size from low-growing plants such as thyme or oregano through shrubs such as witch hazel, wormwood, or box, and creepers such as honeysuckle, to trees, such as the bay or the curry tree. Mankind's extensive history of utilizing herbs provides examples of every part of the plant being valuable. Leaves are probably the part of the herb most often used: for flavoring in cooking, eating as a vegetable, making herbal infusions and for other purposes. Stems, which

Above: Purple loosestrife is native to Europe, Asia, and North Africa and has long been used medicinally.
Below: Lavender has long been valued for both its thereputic properties and for its powerful fragrance.

transport nutrients for the plant, are also used, with lemon grass being an example of a plant stem with a culinary purpose. Flowers, often valued particularly for their fragrance, contain the most active ingredients when they first open fully and are best harvested in dry weather. There are many herb flowers used for a number of different purposes such as teas, cordials, and cosmetics, among them elderflower, camomile, and lavender. Herb seeds are employed in many ways, including flavor (caraway, poppy, or fenugreek), to treat stomach pains (fennel seeds), and oil (safflower). Herb berries include juniper, which famously gives gin its distinctive taste, and elderberries, used to make country wines. Herb roots (the underground part of the plant which absorbs water and nutrients), rhizomes (the underground stem from which roots grow), and bulbs (underground storage organs) are all widely used in different ways. Garlic bulbs, for example, are eaten around the world, valued for their healthy properties as well as their taste. Horseradish roots, with their fiery, pungent flavor, are used as a popular condiment in certain European countries.

Throughout history, all around the globe different cultures have made use of the plants that grew wild around them, with herbs being a wonderful natural resource. A traditional knowledge of the uses and the dangers of the plants that could be found in hedgerows, forests, and fields was helpful, and sometimes invaluable, particularly in the case of medicinal

Above: Many herbs are cultivated by gardeners for their attractive foliage and flowers but popoular culinary herbs such as basil, thyme, and mint are grown commercially to supply the needs of food stores.

herbs. Foraging for herbs in the wild is something that human beings have done for centuries. Today, however, a number of wild herbs that once were abundant are now sadly endangered, including cowslips and pasque flowers. When harvesting herbs from the wild it is important to do so responsibly, picking only a few leaves, flowers, or fruits to make sure that the plant can reproduce and not uprooting or destroying the plant.

The herbs in this reference book have been arranged in alphabetical order by their scientific names. This is to avoid any confusion when it comes to identifying a herb correctly. All plants are classified according to their shared relationships with other plants. The system of scientific names in use today is binomial (that is, using two names) and can be traced back to the Swedish botanist Carl Linnaeus. Each plant is given two Latinized names: the first being the name of the genus (a group of related species) and the second denoting the species (a group of plants that are similar and naturally breed with each other). A plant family is a group of either a single genus or related genera, different mints, for example, belong to the plant family known as Lamiaceae. Hybrids, a cross between two species which usually occurs artificially through cultivation, are shown by the symbol "x."

Herb Gardens

There is a long history of cultivating herbs in gardens of their own, dating back to Ancient Egypt, where herbs were used extensively in temples for rituals and cleansing and so were grown for these purposes. In Islamic cultures, where paradise was imagined as a beautiful, enclosed garden, useful plants were grown within enclosures. Roman villa grounds traditionally included flower gardens, orchards, vineyards, and herb gardens.

In Europe, monasteries played an important part for centuries in maintaining the knowledge of cultivating herbs. St. Benedict, who founded the hugely influential Benedictine monastic order in Monte Cassino, Italy c. AD530, wrote his Rules, a set of precepts for monastic life that have been closely followed since. He ordered that "all the necessaries" for the monks should be available within the monastery walls, emphasizing the importance of the monastery garden.

The sixteenth century saw the rise of the Physic Garden, that is, a garden devoted to plants related to medicine or "physic." Medieval universities created herb gardens for educational purposes: Italy saw the establishment of Europe's first

Botanic Gardens, at Pisa in 1543, Padua in 1545, and at Florence in 1550, each of them designed as medical teaching collections. In 1621 Oxford's Physic Garden was founded, now known as the Oxford Botanic Garden. In 1673 the Chelsea Physic Garden was created in London by the Worshipful Society of Apothecaries in order to teach its apprentices to identify and use plants. The Royal Botanic Gardens at Kew, London, traces its ancestry to a Physic Garden,

Above and opposite: Herb gardens are traditionally well ordered, with geometric beds divided by paths and hedges.

established by Princess Augusta in 1759. Other parts of the world, too, saw the rise of the herb garden. Japan's oldest botanical garden, the Koishikawa Botanical Garden in Tokyo, was originally the Koishikawa Medicinal Herb Garden, founded in 1684 by the Tokugawa Shogunate as a collection of medicinal plants to provide herbal medicines.

The sixteenth century in England also saw the rise of the knot garden, composed of flower beds laid out in intricate, geometric patterns, with each bed defined by low-cut, evergreen hedges. Although not herb gardens as such, these knot gardens often contained many of the fragrant plants that we think of as herbs. The passion for formal gardens continued in the seventeenth and eighteenth centuries in Europe with the fashion for landscape gardening among the aristocracy. Great houses, such as the stately French chateaux, had their formal herb gardens, elegantly laid out in hedge-trimmed beds, performing both an aesthetic and a practical function. On a more humble level, cottage gardens too grew herbs for cookery and for healing purposes. The herb lawn, grown from fragrant, low-growing herbs such as camomile or varieties of thyme, has long been a popular feature of herb gardens. Today, people continue to grow herbs in a variety of ways, from window boxes containing easy-to-grow staples such as parsley, mint, or chives to more classically structured herb gardens.

Herbs in Folklore, Myths, and Legend

With so many herbs used by man since the earliest times, it is not surprising that a number of them feature in myths and legends and have much folklore associated with them. Yarrow stalks were used in foretelling by the druids and in ancient China, and the herb's Latin name, *Achillea millefolium,* refers to its associations with the Greek mythic hero Achilles, who is said to have used yarrow to stanch his warriors' wounds during the Trojan War. Myrtle was held to be sacred to the goddess Aphrodite and used in weddings. Betony, used by the Anglo-Saxons against elf sickness was traditionally planted in churchyards and cemeteries to offer protection against witchcraft. Other herbs with magical associations include mugwort, linked to witchcraft and fertility rituals; witch hazel, traditionally used for divining; and great mullein, thought to drive away evil spirits.

Herbs with Christian associations include angelica: known by Renaissance doctors as "root of the Holy Ghost" and linked to angels, it was thought to offer protection against witches. Basil was said to have grown round Christ's tomb after the Resurrection and was seen as a herb of love. Rosemary's blue flowers are said to owe their shade and fragrance to the Virgin Mary throwing her cloak over the bush, changing the previously white blossoms to the color of her cloak. In Christian folklore the Virgin Mary's milk ran down the leaves of the milk thistle (also known as the blessed thistle), creating its striking white-patterned leaves.

Below: With its pretty flowers, many varieties of thyme are valued by gardeners as ground cover rather than for their culinary uses.
Opposite: Basil is traditionally associated with love.

Herbal Knowledge

Knowledge of herbs, their properties and their perils has been passed down both orally and in written form for centuries, sometimes for millennia. Among the cultures with a venerable history of using herbs medicinally for thousands of years are the ancient Chinese and the Indians with Ayurvedic medicine. At some point during the Han dynasty in China (206 BC–AD 220), a seminal book on Chinese pharmacology

was written known as the *Shen Nong Canon of Herbs*, attributed to the legendary emperor Shen Nong. From Ancient Egypt comes the Ebers papyrus (c.1500 BC), one of the oldest preserved medical documents, which records the use of herbs including wormwood. In classical times a number of important texts were written, including two botanical treatises written by the Greek philosopher Theophrastus around 300 BC *Historia Plantarum* (*Enquiry into Plants*) and *De Causis Plantarum* (*Growth of Plants*). In AD 77 Pliny the Elder, a Roman natural historian, wrote *Historia Naturalis* (*Natural History*) which included the medical uses of herbs. In AD100 a Greek physician named Dioscorides wrote *De Materia Medica*, listing 950 curative substances of which 600 are from plants. Each entry contained a drawing and description of the plant, an outline of its medicinal qualities and method of preparation as well as warnings about any undesirable effects. This hugely influential herbal remained a standard reference book in western society until around AD 1600. About fifty years after Dioscorides' landmark work, the Greek physician Galen produced *De Simplibus*, another hugely influential medical book, laying out the theory of the 'humors'. The great Islamic physician Abd Allah Ibn Sina (known also as Avicenna) wrote his encyclopaedic *Canon of Medicine* around AD 1000, drawing on Galen's work.

Until the fifteenth century European herbals were manuscripts handwritten in Latin, which only a few people could read. With the invention of printing in 1440 and the move from writing in Latin to writing in the vernacular, there was a rise in the number of herbals. In 1570 a Swiss alchemist known as

Paracelsus published a herbal explaining the Doctrine of Signatures, which said that healing herbs had signs in their appearance given by God to indicate their use. For centuries European herbalism was influenced by Paracelsus's Doctrine. After European explorers and colonizers discovered the "New World" of the Americas, a Spanish physician and botanist, Nicolas Monardes, produced the first American herbal in 1569, translated into English as *Joyfull News Out of the Newe Founde Worlde*. In the late sixteenth century the herbalist and gardener John Gerard wrote one of the first herbals to be written entirely in English, *The Herball or Generall Historie of Plants*, still referred to. In 1652 the astrologer and herbalist Nicholas Culpeper produced, *The English Physician, or an Astrologo-Physical Discourse of the Vulgar Herbs of this Nation*. This book, in which Culpepper drew upon the Doctrine of Signatures and his knowledge of astrology as well as herbs, was to be hugely successful, becoming one of the best-selling herbals of all time.

Culinary Herbs

Since man's early history, herbs have been used to add flavor to food. A few herbs are widely used around the world. Garlic, for example, with its powerful odor and taste, is used almost universally, a feature of many cuisines including Chinese, Indian, European, and Middle Eastern.

Opposite: German camomile.
Above: An illustration of calendula based on those from De Materia Medica *by Pedanios Dioscorides.*

Certain herbs, however, are particularly associated with specific cuisines. Indian cuisine is famous for its use of spices, but alongside these a number of herbs are widely used. Fresh coriander, for example, is blended with green chillies and lemon juice to make a zingy, piquant fresh chutney. Fresh mint is also used in North Indian cookery to make chutneys, flavor appetizers and, traditionally, rice pilaf dishes. A herb which is particularly characteristic of South Indian cuisine is the curry leaf, from the curry tree, which adds a particular spiciness and slight bitterness to dishes including curries, chutneys, and pickles. It is added as an aromatic to these dishes but not eaten.

In European cookery, certain herbs are widely used in a number of countries while others are particularly redolent of specific cuisines. Basil, for example, with its strong, sweet scent, evokes Italian cuisine, famously a key ingredient of pesto, the Genoese sauce made from fresh basil, pine nuts, garlic, olive oil, and grated Parmesan cheese, traditionally served with *trenette* pasta. Dill is associated with Scandinavia, often used in fish in with dishes such as Sweden's famous gravadlax (salmon marinated with rock salt, dill, lemon, sugar, and pepper). Aromatic bay leaves are one of the most widely used herbs in European and North American kitchens, added to stews, sauces, and marinades. Rosemary crops up across Europe, combined with lamb in many countries, as its sharp aroma cuts across the meat's fattiness. In classical French cookery, certain combinations of herbs are traditional, such as *fines herbes*, (chopped parsley, chervil, tarragon, and chives),

herbes de Provence (thyme, rosemary, bay, basil, and savory) and *bouquets garni*, a herb bundle usually consisting of parsley, thyme, and bay leaves. In Britain, popular culinary herbs include curly parsley, chives, and mint, with the latter added to new potatoes and peas, or made into mint sauce. Strong-flavored sage is classically used in stuffings or to season sausages and cheese.

In China, garlic is the herb most widely used, adding flavor to dishes from stir-fries to slow-braised hot-pots. Fresh coriander crops up as a garnish and in dishes such as beef or fish soup. Chinese chives, with their robust, garlic-like taste, are treated as a vegetable rather than a herb.

In the Middle East, flat-leafed parsley is a key flavoring in its own right rather than a garnish, taking center stage particularly in dishes such as Lebanese tabbouleh, a refreshing salad made from finely-chopped flat-leafed parsley, bulgur wheat, and tomato.

In South-east Asian kitchens, lemon grass, with its citrus flavor is a key ingredient. Glossy green kaffir lime leaves are often added whole to

Above: Applemint, one of the many varieties of mint which include spearmint and pepermint.
Below: Garlic is an important herb in both eastern and western cultures.
Opposite: Parsely, one of the classic French "fines herbes."

recipes, adding a particular fragrance to dishes such as tom yum goong, a chilli-hot and sour Thai prawn soup. Fresh coriander features in Thai cooking, and the Thais

also use the plant's roots, crushed with garlic and pepper, to flavor meat and fish.

Many herbs that were traditionally enjoyed as salad leaves or a green vegetable are no longer eaten in that way. Certain herbs, however, are still popularly consumed as salad leaves, such as dandelion leaves, eaten in France and purslane, in the Middle East. Perhaps the best-known salad herb these days is rocket or arugula, now widely used in the Northern Hemisphere as a fashionable salad leaf.

Herbs also feature in confectionery. The mint family, with its cool, refreshing taste, has long been used in in the preparation of sweet foods. Liquorice sweets derive their characteristic taste from the roots of *Glycyrhiza glabra*, and are hugely popular around the world, ranging from salty liquorice favored by the Dutch, Germans, and Scandinavians to the sweeter confection preferred by the Americans, Australians, and British. Aniseed seeds are another herb traditionally used in sweets, often in *dragée* form such as sugar-coated aniseed balls. Herbs that aid digestion sometimes feature in sweet form, with sugar-coated fennel seeds being a traditional post-prandial digestive in India. In North America, oil of wintergreen was a traditional flavoring for both confectionery, such as candy sticks, and cough drops.

Herbs in Drinks

There is a long tradition of herbs being used in drinks. Herb teas made with fresh or dried leaves and flowers, of course, are the classic way of using herbs, with teas such as mint, bergamot, or camomile enjoyed for their flavor as well as their digestive and soothing properties. In rural communities it used to be the custom to make herb wines and beers, a practical way of making the most of the flowers and plants found growing in the countryside. Herbs used for these drinks were wide-ranging including nettles, meadowsweet, cowslips, dandelions, and primroses, with the wine made from spring flowers matured and drunk at Christmas time. Cordials, sweetened syrups, were another traditional way of using herbs and elderflower cordial, with its noticeable muscat fragrance, is today enjoying a revival in Britain. In Germany sweet woodruff is traditionally added to Rhine wine to make a celebratory May Day tipple called *Maibowle*. Gin, originally

from Holland, is flavored with aromatic juniper. A number of liqueurs are flavored with herbs, with angelica seeds, for example, being used in Chartreuse liqueur and hyssop the main flavoring. Many bitter herbs are used this way, with oil of wormwood being a key ingredient of the notorious, addictive alcoholic apéritif absinthe, once hugely fashionable in France and banned in that country in 1915.

Herbs in Medicine
For centuries, all around the world, herbs have been used for healing and treatment. With many herbs growing widely in the wild, these plants were an invaluable form of free medicine, available to those who knew how to use them. Medicinal herbs were also deliberately cultivated for use by specialist practitioners.

Above: Many people consider herbal teas to be a soothing alternative to traditional Indian tea.
Right: Borage flowers are a pretty addition to summer drinks.
Opposite: Rosehips are high in vitamin C and can be used to make herbal teas as well as jams and jellies.

Indian Ayurvedic medicine views health as being a harmony between body, mind, and spirit. This system of medicine uses herbs extensively. A key Ayurvedic medicinal treatise is the *Charaka Samhita*, consisting of knowledge passed down orally from the seventh century BC and written down in the first century AD, which mentions around 350 herbal medicines. The herbs are used in a huge variety of forms, including the fresh juice, crushed, or powdered herbs and herbs cooked in oil, butter, or sugar.

China, too, has a venerable history of using herbs medicinally. Traditional Chinese medicine draws on the idea of opposite cosmic forces, known as yin and yang, and the five elements (fire, metal, water, wood, and earth), with the five organs corresponding to these elements. Herbs in this form of medicine are classified according to the six tastes as pungent, sweet, sour, bitter, salty, or bland, with each taste having a particular use in treatment. A seminal textbook was Li Shizhen's *Compendium of Materia Medica'*, compiled in 1578 during the Ming dynasty, a 53-volume work which is still referred to today. In it he described 1892 herbs, giving their uses. There are, however, fifty so-called "fundamental herbs" at the heart of traditional Chinese medicine, tailored cocktails of different herbs used to treat each individual patient.

In the west, much herbal knowledge was passed down from the Ancient Greeks and Romans. The Arabs also added considerably to herbal knowledge, with one essential Arab contribution being the separation of essential oils from herbs by the process of distillation. During the Middle Ages, the healing powers of herbs was an area of knowledge nurtured for centuries by the Christian monasteries. The Middle Ages then saw the rise of the apothecaries, who became specialists in making up herbal medications.

Twentieth-century France saw the development of aromatherapy, the use of essential oils for health. Scented oils were used by many historic cultures, such as the Ancient Egyptians, but the term was coined in 1928 by a French chemist and perfumier named René-Maurice Gattefosse, who discovered the healing powers of lavender oil by chance when he burned his own hand. Gattefosse's work was expanded upon some years later by French army doctor Jean Valnet, who used essential oils to treat soldiers wounded in World War II. Today, aromatherapy and Bach Flower Remedies, the use of flower essences developed in the 1930s by Dr. Edward Bach, both enjoy a popular following.

In North America, the Native American tribes had an extensive knowledge of the healing properties of the plants around them and some European settlers drew upon this source of information. An important movement in North America's use of herbs was founded by one Samuel Thomson, whose dangerously ill wife was cured through traditional herbal remedies. This cure inspired Johnson to develop a series of treatments, drawing on Native American herbal treatments, known as the "Thomsonian System" of medicine and in 1822 he wrote his popular *New Guide to Health or Botanic Family Physician*. The 1830s in North America saw the foundation of the Eclectic Medical Institute, a term coined by a doctor living among Native Americans, which promoted the use of medicinal herbs. One group of Americans that did much to make plant medicines available was the Shaker sect, who developed wholesale herb-selling, initially gathering them from the wild, then cultivating herbs themselves on a large scale, producing their first catalogue of medical herbs in 1830.

Throughout human history, herbs have been prepared in various different ways for medicinal purposes. Herbal infusions, taken internally, are made by steeping fresh or dried herbs in hot water, an easy and accessible way to use these plants, especially their leaves and flowers. Decoctions, made from roots, bark, and berries, involve actively boiling the herb. Tinctures are made by steeping herbs in alcohol, a process which preserves the herb

Right: Scented candles as well as essential oils are used in aromatherapy.
Opposite: Both the flowers and the leaves of wormwood are used in the manufacture of absinthe.

in a potent and portable form. Sweetened herbal syrups are a way of making bitter or unpleasant-tasting herbs more palatable, preserving them, and also making a preparation which is soothing for the throat. Ointments, made from herbs dissolved in an oil or fat, are applied externally and form a protective layer on the skin. Creams, made from emulsions of water and oil or fat mixed with dissolved herbs, are also applied externally and become partly absorbed into the skin. Poultices, moist pastes or pulp of herbs, are applied warm to the skin, used to treat skin problems, aches, and pains. Compresses are cloths soaked in a strained herbal infusion or wash and applied to the skin to soothe it.

Today in the West herbal medicine is enjoying something of a revival, no longer dismissed as mere foolish superstition or custom. One only has to visit a chemist to see how many traditional herbal medicines are widely available, from echinacea capsules to boost the immune system to St John's wort, a popular treatment for depression. Research has shown that many of the plants used in traditional herbal medicine do indeed contain components that are effective treatments. Feverfew for example, recommended by the seventeenth-century herbalist Culpeper for "all pains in the head," has been clinically shown to reduce the frequency, severity, and duration of migraines. Milk thistle, historically used to treat liver diseases, contains silymarin, a complex of flavonoids found to be effective in protecting the liver from toxic damage. There is a misconception that because herbs are a "natural" remedy they cannot be harmful. *Taken correctly, and in consultation with a knowledgeable practitioner when necessary, herbs undoubtedly have many healing powers. However, many herbs can have dangerous side-effects if not used correctly and historically herbal practitioners have always known that herbs can damage as well as heal.*

Toxic Herbs

So used are we to thinking of herbs as healing plants, that it can come as something of a surprise to realize that several herbs are, in fact, very toxic. Despite their deadly properties, however, a number of these herbs are used medicinally for healing purposes. One such herb is the foxglove, an attractive but highly dangerous plant. An English physician, William Withering, having learnt that it was used in a traditional herbal remedy for dropsy, became convinced that the plant could be efficacious in the treatment of heart disease and in 1785 published *An Account of the Foxglove* laying out its healing qualities. We now know that foxglove contains cardiac glycosides which help the heart to beat more strongly and more slowly with digitalin, from the common foxglove, a standard medical treatment. The opium poppy, despite being poisonous, was used as a narcotic for centuries. It contains the alkalines morphine and codeine, potent painkillers and sedatives still used today, but also highly addictive. Deadly nightshade, while known as a poison, was used as an anaesthetic and also as a cosmetic during medieval times. Atropine, the poisonous alkaloid it contains, is used today for surgery and medical eye examinations. Monkshood, although a highly toxic herb, was thought to be an antidote to other poisons, particularly to snake venom. Henbane, another famous poison, was also used as a sedative, with the first-century Greek physician Dioscorides administering it to induce sleep. It was a notorious poison, with Hamlet's father in Shakespeare's play killed by a distillation of henbane poured into his ear as he sleeps. It was also used in real life by the infamous poisoner Dr Crippen in 1910 to kill his wife.

Opposite: Despite its delicate appearance, the opium poppy is the source of a powerful drug.
Below: The castor oil plant was used as a purgative but the seeds are highly toxic if eaten.

Above: Potpourri is made with dried herbs but they can also be used to create wedding confetti.
Opposite right: Calendula oil is extracted from marigold petals to make skin creams.
Opposite left: Heartsease was used in the treatment of eczema.

Preserving Herbs

Drying has long been a way of preserving herbs. Many culinary herbs, such as bay or oregano, keep their flavor well when dried or even have it enhanced by the drying process, so are traditionally used in dried form as well as fresh. The purpose of drying is to preserve the essential oils while driving out the plant's water content.

Fresh culinary herbs can also usefully be frozen, a process which works well with soft-leafed herbs such as mint or parsley, retaining their flavor, color and vitamins. Herbs that have been frozen can be used directly in cooking, with no thawing necessary.

Another popular, traditional way of preserving the flavor of herbs is to add them to oils or vinegars, used in their turn for salad dressings, sauces, or marinades.

Potpourri, a fragrant mixture of dried flowers and herbs, is a good way of using dried herbs. The term derives from the French for 'rotten pot', being originally a moist mixture of pickled flowers and leaves. Rose petals and lavender flowers are staple ingredients, while fragrant herbs such as mints, sage, lemon verbena, and rosemary are also popular. Certain herb flowers, including calendula and tansy, keep their color well when dried. Ground aromatic orris is a traditional fixative in potpourris. Herbal essential oils are a simple way of adding fragrance to the mixture. Potpourri displayed in a pretty bowl both looks attractive and scents the air around it.

Cosmetic Herbs

Herbs have been used in beauty products for centuries for a variety of purposes: adding fragrance, cleansing the body and treating blemishes. Perfumed oils scented with herbs were used in Ancient Egypt, India, and Persia and the use of perfumes in a variety of forms continued to be popular in classical Greece and Rome, where bath-houses played an important part in society. The Arab discovery in the Middle Ages of how to distil essential herbal oils was an important breakthrough in their use in fragrances.

Certain herbs were valued for their astringent properties, such as yarrow, used to treat greasy hair or oily skin. Rosemary was traditionally added to a tonic rinse to add lustrer to dull hair and against dandruff. It was also used in Queen of Hungary water, an early toilet water dating back to the fourteenth century. On the other hand, marsh mallow, with its mucilaginous roots, was valued for its soothing properties, used for dry skin or chapped hands. The roots and leaves of the wild strawberry were also seen as cooling, recommended by the seventeenth-century herbalist Nicholas Culpeper "to take away any redness in the face, or spots, or other deformities in the skin, and to make it clear and smooth."

Baths have historically been perfumed by the addition of herbal infusions or decoctions. Aromatic, strong-smelling lavender, with its generic name deriving from the Latin verb 'to wash' and its antiseptic properties, has a long and particular association with cleansing, traditionally used in soothing baths to relax muscles and also in perfumery.

The cosmetic uses of herbs are varied and ingenious: horsetail, high in silica, is a traditional treatment for brittle fingernails. Camomile is used in a rinse to lighten fair hair, elder to reduce freckles, and marigold petal infusions to treat eczema and acne. The mint family, long used to freshen breath, is today widely used in toothpastes. One particularly curious practice during medieval times was the use of the juice of deadly nightshade to dilate the pupils of women's eyes, making them appear large and lustrous.

HERBS

ENGLISH MACE ACHILLEA AGERATUM

OTHER NAMES: Garden mace, maudlin, sweet milfoil, sweet Nancy
PLANT FAMILY: Asteraceae
HEIGHT: 12–18in
HABIT: Hardy perennial with narrow, deeply serrated, bright green leaves and clusters of small, cream flowers
HABITAT: Well-drained soil in sun
USES: Culinary, medicinal, decorative

Native to Switzerland, English mace is cultivated in Northern Europe, though it is something of a rarity. Its generic name *Achillea* refers to Achilles, the hero of Greek mythology, who is reputed to have been taught the medicinal uses of herbs by the centaur Chiron. Medicinally, it was traditionally taken internally to treat stomach disorders. As a culinary herb, its mildly aromatic leaves can be used to flavor stuffing for roast chicken, added to soups, or sprinkled over pasta, rice, or potato dishes. Its pretty flowers can be dried and incorporated into dried flower arrangements; it is also an ornamental herb to grow by gardeners.

ACHILLEA MILLEFOLIUM YARROW

Found growing wild in wasteland and meadows in many parts of the world, including Asia, Europe, and North America, yarrow has a venerable history as a medicinal herb. Its Latin name refers to the mythical Greek warrior Achilles, who applied yarrow to stanch the wounds of his warriors during the Trojan War. Other traditional medicinal uses for yarrow were to reduce heavy menstruation and against cold and flu. Yarrow infusions are also added to shampoos to treat greasy hair. As well as its many reputed medicinal properties, yarrow is a plant with magical associations; yarrow stalks were used by the ancient Chinese for foretelling and the druids for divining. Although its culinary applications are limited, young yarrow leaves can be added to salads.

OTHER NAMES: Carpenter's weed, millefoil, nose-bleed, soldier's woundwort

PLANT FAMILY: Compositae

HEIGHT: Up to 3ft

HABIT: Hardy perennial with green, feathery fernlike leaves and flat heads of tiny, pink-tinged white flowers

HABITAT: Waysides and fields in a sunny position

USES: Culinary, medicinal, cosmetic

MONKSHOOD ACONITUM NAPELLUS

OTHER NAMES: Wolf's
bane, friar's cap
PLANT FAMILY:
Ranunculaceae
HEIGHT: 4—5ft
HABIT: Hardy perennial
with deeply lobed,
green leaves and tall
spires of deep blue
flowers
HABITAT: Moist soil in the
shade, such as stream
banks or ditches
USES: Medicinal

Despite its attractive appearance, monkshood has long
been known as a highly poisonous plant, with all parts of
the plant from the roots to the leaves being dangerous.
In Greek mythology, it was rumored to have sprung
from the spittle dropped from the jaws of Cerberus, the
monstrous three-headed dog that guarded the gates of
Hades. It has long been mentioned in herbals both as a
source of poison and also as an antidote against other
poisons, particularly snake venom. Gardeners growing
monkshood should wear gloves when handling it. The
name "monkshood" is a reference to the hooded, deep
blue, delphinium-like flowers, which allow the plant to
be pollinated only by bees.

AGASTACHE FOENICULUM ANISE HYSSOP

Native to North America, this herb was introduced into Europe only in the nineteenth century. As its common name suggests, it has a notable aniseed scent and flavor. Its fragrant leaves are added to salads and also used to make a herbal infusion or added to summer fruit cups. Its summer spikes of flowers are a good source of nectar, notably attractive to butterflies and bees. It is, therefore, a popular plant with North American bee-keepers, producing a fine, anise-flavored honey. Growing in neat clumps, it is popular as an ornamental addition to herb gardens. Medicinally it was used by Native Americans to treat coughs.

OTHER NAMES: Anise mint, giant hyssop, fennel hyssop
PLANT FAMILY: Labiatae
HEIGHT: Up to 2ft
HABIT: Hardy perennial with pointed, ovate, mid-green, toothed leaves and spikes of small, light purple flowers
HABITAT: Free-draining, rich soil
USES: Culinary, decorative, medicinal

AGRIMONY

AGRIMONIA EUPATORIA

Found growing wild throughout Europe in fields, hedgerows, and waste ground, agrimony has long been valued for its medicinal properties. Its name is thought to come from the Greek *agremone* which means "plant that can heal diseases of the eye," while *eupatoria* in its Latin name is a reference to the first-century King Mithridates VI Eupator, renowned for his knowledge of herbal medicines. Its distinctive burrs are alluded to in its common names. Over the centuries, notable herbalists have recommended agrimony as a purgative and a treatment for liver complaints, and for curing sores, wounds, and coughs. It has a high tannin content and consequently has an astringent action. Its dried leaves and flowers are used as the base for mouth gargles, tonics, and dressings.

OTHER NAMES: Cockleburr, sticklewort
PLANT FAMILY: Rosaceae
HEIGHT: Up to 3ft
HABIT: Hardy perennial with downy leaves, divided into leaflets and long spikes of small, yellow flowers
HABITAT: Well-drained soil in sunshine
USES: Medicinal, culinary

BUGLE

AJUGA REPTANS

Native to Europe, North Africa, and West
Asia, this fast-growing perennial thrives in
damp woods and grassy fields. The famous
seventeenth-century herbalist Culpeper
valued it highly in treating wounds and also
as a cure for hangovers. Its astringent
properties have made it a traditional
homeopathic treatment for throat irritations
and mouth ulcers, with its leaves used both
fresh and dried. Gardeners value the fact
that it provides good ground cover, often
growing it at border edges or underneath
shrubs, and it is also popular with bees and
butterflies. A bronze-leafed form, known as
bronze bugle, is particularly popular as an
ornamental plant.

PLANT FAMILY: Lamiaceae
HEIGHT: 4—12in
HABIT: Evergreen perennial, with oval to spoon-shaped
leaves and whorled spikes of purplish-blue flowers
HABITAT: Moist soil in sun or partial shade
USES: Medicinal, decorative

LADY'S MANTLE
ALCHEMILLA XANHOCHLORA (ALCHEMILLA VULGARIS)

OTHER NAMES: Bear's foot, lion's foot, nine hooks, Our Lady's mantle
PLANT FAMILY: Rosaceae
HEIGHT: 12in
HABIT: Hardy perennial with kidney-shaped, indented, toothed green leaves and clusters of small yellow-green flowers
HABITAT: Full sun to partial shade and rich soil
USES: Medicinal

Native to Europe, this hardy plant thrives in a range of conditions, from damp grassland to mountain ledges. Its Latin name derives from the Arabic *alchimia*, meaning "alchemy," reflecting a belief in the plant's magical properties. Herbalists reputedly gathered the drops of early morning dew which lay in the herb's kidney-shaped leaves for use in potions. The common name is inspired by the characteristic mantle shape of the leaf and also reflects the ancient tradition of using this plant to treat women's menstrual problems. The herb's nickname was indeed "woman's best friend."
Medicinally, lady's mantle was also employed to treat bleeding wounds and as a heart tonic and diuretic. Its dried leaves are used in infusions while its fresh leaves can be applied as a poultice. Today it is often planted as an ornamental plant, as an edging for borders.

JACK-BY-THE-HEDGE
ALLIARIA PETIOLATA

Native to Europe and temperate Asia, this hardy herb grows well in damp, shady places, such as hedgerows and wood edges. Both the leaves and stalk emit an unmistakable garlic smell when crushed, hence its popular names "garlic mustard" or "hedge garlic." Historically, jack-by-the-hedge has long been used for both medicinal and culinary purposes. It was taken internally to treat bronchitis and asthma and applied externally to relieve bites and stings and to treat minor injuries. Believed to add digestion, its young leaves were used as a potherb, adding a mild garlic flavor to soups or stews, or finely chopped and added to salads.

OTHER NAMES: Garlic mustard, hedge garlic
PLANT FAMILY: Brassicaceae
HEIGHT: 1—4ft
HABIT: Hardy perennial with heart-shaped, toothed, bright green leaves and flat-topped clusters of small white flowers
HABITAT: Moist soil in shade or sun
USES: Culinary, medicinal

GARLIC

ALLIUM SATIVUM

Mankind's use of garlic's strong-smelling bulbs goes back several millennia, making garlic one of the world's oldest herbs. Its use is chronicled in Babylonian times, over 5000 years ago, while the Ancient Egyptians thought it imparted strength and the Ancient Romans ate it before going into battle. Thought to originate from Asia, garlic is widely grown and used around the world. It has historically been valued for its medicinal properties, with its first mention in Chinese traditional medicine around 500AD. Its antiseptic properties have long been recognized and its juice was extracted to treat the wounds of soldiers in World War I. Today, garlic is valued for its ability to reduce low-density lipoproteins ("bad" cholesterol) and is the subject of much scientific research. As a culinary herb, garlic is used in myriad ways, adding its full-bodied flavor to salad dressings, stews, curry pastes, pasta sauces, stir-fries, and many other dishes. There is much folklore attached to garlic, most famously that it kept off vampires.

PLANT FAMILY: Liliaceae
HEIGHT: 16—24in
HABIT: Hardy perennial with long, narrow, flat green leaves and a spherical pink or white flowerhead
HABITAT: Prefers full sun and rich, well-drained soil
USES: Culinary, medicinal

CHIVES

ALLIUM SCHOENOPRASUM

A well-known culinary herb, chives was introduced into Britain by the Romans. The common name is derived from the Latin *cepa,* which means onion, a clue to its mild onion taste. The Latin name is from *schoenus,* for "a rush or sedge," a reference to its reed-like appearance and during the Middle Ages it was called "rush-leek." Because of its delicate flavor and texture chives is used fresh and raw rather than cooked, particularly in egg dishes such as omelettes or scrambled eggs. Bright green, finely snipped chives is a popular garnish, sprinkled over soups or soured cream, for example. Both the leaves and the pretty, edible flowers can be added to salads. Medicinally, chives was valued for its stimulant effect on the appetite and as an aid to digestion.

PLANT FAMILY: Liliaceae
HEIGHT: 9in
HABIT: Hardy perennial with long, slender, grass-like green leaves and globular clusters of tiny purple flowers
HABITAT: Tolerant of most soils, with moist, well-drained soil ideal
USES: Culinary, medicinal

CHINESE CHIVES ALLIUM TUBEROSUM

OTHER NAME: Garlic chives
PLANT FAMILY: Liliaceae
HEIGHT: 16in
HABIT: Hardy perennial with long, flat, slender, grass-like green leaves and heads of dainty, star-shaped white flowers
HABITAT: Rich, well-drained soil in full sun
USES: Culinary, medicinal

Native to South-East Asia, this strongly-scented herb has long been used in Chinese cuisine but has only more recently been cultivated in Europe. As its common name "garlic chives" suggests, the thick, flat leaves possess a pungent garlic scent and a mild garlic flavor. Its primary use is as a culinary herb in China, adding a distinctive taste to dumplings and braised dishes. Robust enough to stand up to being cooked, it is popular in stir-fries. Blanched Chinese chives, grown in the dark, is also popular in Chinese cuisine, traditionally added to noodle dishes or spring rolls. Containing a sulfur-rich mustard oil, Chinese chives is thought to aid digestion and promote the flow of blood. Its antiseptic qualities meant that in ancient China it was reputedly fed to prisoners who had been flogged, to aid healing.

ALLIUM URSINUM RAMSONS

Native to Europe and Asia, ramsons is found growing wild in damp woodland, along streams, and in shady places. As its many common names suggest, the plant possesses a distinctive, pungent garlic scent. The name "ramsons" derives from the Old English *hramson*, meaning "wild garlic." Medicinally, the freshly pressed juice of ramsons was used to treat coughs, sore throats, and colds. In the kitchen its leaves added flavor to salads, sauces, and egg dishes. In Britain it is currently enjoying something of a revival as a fashionable hedgerow food.

OTHER NAMES: Badger's garlic, bear's garlic, devil's garlic, gypsy onion, stinking Jenny, wild garlic, wood garlic

PLANT FAMILY: Liliaceae

HEIGHT: 12—18in

HABIT: Hardy perennial with spear-shaped, dark green, glossy leaves and heads of six-petalled white flowers

HABITAT: Moist soil in semi to full shade

USES: Culinary, medicinal

ALOE VERA

ALOE VERA (ALOE BARBADENSIS)

Native to Southern Africa, this architectural plant, with its striking foliage, is now a popular houseplant in countries with cooler climates. It has long been valued for its medicinal properties, with the Ancient Egyptians using it to treat catarrh. It was so prized that Alexander the Great is said to have conquered the island of Socotra in the Indian Ocean so that his soldiers could benefit from the wound-healing properties of the aloes growing on the island. Its succulent leaves contain a gel (obtained simply by breaking off a leaf and cutting it open) which can be spread directly on cuts and minor burns where it both soothes and stimulates the healing process. It is still valued medicinally, with the gel from its leaves being harvested and sold fresh or evaporated for use in creams, lotions, pills, and tinctures.

OTHER NAME: Barbados aloe
PLANT FAMILY: Aloaceae
HEIGHT: 2ft
HABIT: Tender perennial with rosettes of succulent gray-green, spiked, pointed foliage and bell-shaped yellow or orange flowers on a stem
HABITAT: Sun and well-drained soil
USES: Medicinal

LEMON VERBENA ALOYSIA TRIPHYLLA

PLANT FAMILY: Verbenaceae
HEIGHT: 3—10ft
HABIT: Half-hardy deciduous perennial with long, oval green leaves and tiny pale lilac to white flowers
HABITAT: Prefers a sunny spot with light, well-drained soil
USES: Culinary, medicinal, cosmetic

Introduced to Europe from Chile in the late eighteenth century, this citrus-scented herb has become a popular ornamental plant. It thrives best in its native South America, where it reaches impressive heights not attained in temperate climates. Its essential oil, with its strong lemon fragrance, has long been widely used in the perfume and cosmetics industry. As its dried leaves retain their fragrance well it is a popular component for potpourris. Medicinally, lemon verbena was valued for its mild sedative properties and for relieving spasms. As a culinary herb, its most common use is in refreshing lemon verbena tea, made from fresh or dried leaves. It can also be added to fish dishes, vinegars, jellies, soft drinks, and fruit salads.

ALTHAEA OFFICINALIS MARSH MALLOW

Found throughout Western Europe, Central Asia, and North Africa, the marsh mallow, as its common name suggest, thrives in damp conditions and can cope with water-logged soil, growing wild in marshland. Its generic name *Althaea* comes from the Greek word *altho*, "to cure" and it has a long history as a healing plant, with the Roman natural historian Pliny commending it. The plant's high mucilage content, particularly present in the root, has softening and healing properties, and can be taken internally to treat coughs, sore throats, and stomach ulcers. In cosmetics, mallow is used as a soothing skin toner and a dry hair rinse. Valued by the Romans as a vegetable, its mucilaginous roots were once the basis for the confection marshmallow. The French traditionally eat its young leaves in salads to stimulate the kidneys.

OTHER NAMES:
Mortification root, sweet weed, white mallow

PLANT FAMILY: Malvaceae

HEIGHT: 2—4ft

HABIT: Hardy perennial with velvety, toothed, lobed green leaves and pink or white five-petalled flowers

HABITAT: Prefers full sun and light damp to wet soil

USES: Culinary, medicinal, cosmetic

DILL ANETHUM GRAVEOLENS

OTHER NAMES: Dillseed, dillweed

PLANT FAMILY: Umbelliferae

HEIGHT: 2—3ft

HABIT: Hardy annual with fine, feathery green fronds and flattened clusters of tiny yellow flowers followed by buff-colored, oval seeds

HABITAT: Prefers full sun and well-drained soil

USES: Culinary, medicinal

This dainty herb derives its name from the Old Nordic *dilla,* meaning "to lull," with dill seed being one of the main ingredients in gripe water, used to soothe fretful babies. The seventeenth-century English herbalist Culpeper wrote of it being employed to treat flatulence and hiccups, and it was long regarded as a medicinal herb. Today, we think of it primarily as a culinary herb and use both its delicately flavored leaves and caraway-flavored seeds in the kitchen. Dill seeds are often an ingredient in pickles, especially pickled cucumbers, known as "dill pickles" in North America, and in cabbage dishes such as sauerkraut and coleslaw. In Nordic countries, dill's clean, refreshing flavor is often added to cut through sour cream or yoghurt. Much loved by the Scandinavians, one of its best-known uses is in gravadlax, made by marinating fresh salmon with salt, sugar, pepper, and finely chopped dill leaves.

ANGELICA ARCHANGELICA ANGELICA

As its name suggests, this large, handsome herb has long, but mysterious, heavenly associations. Medieval herbalists called it *herba angelica*, meaning "angelic plant," while Renaissance doctors named it "root of the Holy Ghost." One piece of folklore says that it flowers on the feast day of Michael the Archangel, May 8, hence its name. Another legend tells of an angel who revealed the herb's protective qualities in a dream, and a piece of angelica root held in the mouth was thought to protect against the plague. During the Middle Ages it was thought to offer protection against witches and spells. Today its fragrant essential oil is used in aromatherapy, perfumes, and colognes. While the seeds are added to Chartreuse liqueur, angelica is best-known in culinary terms for the use of its candied stalk and leaf stem in cake decoration.

OTHER NAMES: Archangel, garden angelica, root of the holy ghost

PLANT FAMILY: Umbelliferae

HEIGHT: 3—8ft

HABIT: Hardy biennial with thick, hollow stalks, large, glossy, divided green leaves, and globe-shaped clusters of tiny yellow-green flowers

HABITAT: Sun or partial shade and rich, moist soil

USES: Culinary, cosmetic

CHERVIL

ANTHRISCUS CEREFOLIUM

According to Pliny the Elder (writing in the first century AD) chervil was first cultivated in Syria. There it was eaten as a vegetable, but the Ancient Romans used it as a flavor-adding herb. During the Middle Ages it was valued for its medicinal qualities, prescribed to cleanse the liver and kidneys. Thought of as a "spring tonic" or cleansing herb, it was one of the herbs traditionally eaten during Lent. When it comes to culinary uses, chervil, with its delicate aniseed flavor, is best used fresh rather than dried. It is particularly valued in France where it is one of the traditional *fines herbes* (a mixture of chopped fresh herbs used in cooking) and features in *Béarnaise* or *ravigote* sauces.

PLANT FAMILY: Umbelliferae
HEIGHT: 12—24in
HABIT: Hardy biennial (often grown as an annual) with hollow, lined stems, delicate, bright, lacy leaves, and clusters of tiny white flowers
HABITAT: Partial shade and rich, moisture-retentive soil
USES: Culinary, medicinal

WILD CELERY APIUM GRAVEOLENS

OTHER NAME: Smallage
PLANT FAMILY: Umbelliferae
HEIGHT: Up to 3ft
HABIT: Hardy biennial with solid grooved stems, lobed and toothed green leaves and clusters of tiny green-white flowers
HABITAT: Prefers full sun and rich, well-drained soil
USES: Culinary, medicinal

Native to Europe, North Africa, and South-West Asia, this hedgerow plant has a pronounced celery smell and a strong, bitter taste. It has been in use since ancient times and is mentioned in Ancient Egyptian texts and in Homer's *Odyssey*. The Latin name *graveolens,* meaning "strong-smelling" is a reference to its characteristic, powerfully aromatic scent. Because of its powerful taste it was used primarily as a flavoring. Cultivated celery, *Apium graveolens* var. *dulce,* with its milder flavor allowing it to be eaten as a vegetable, was developed from wild celery during the seventeenth century in France and Italy. Medicinally, wild celery was eaten to treat indigestion and loss of appetite and to reduce blood pressure.

ARCTIUM LAPPA BURDOCK

This tall, robust herb, native to Europe and West Asia but also found in North America, grows in waste ground and by roadsides. Its characteristic hooked burrs are the reason for its generic name, from the Greek *arktos* for "bear" and the Latin *lappa* meaning "burr." Traditionally popular with children for playing with, the burrs were nicknamed "beggar's buttons." There is a long history of using burdock medicinally, and in both Chinese and western medicine it was highly regarded as blood-cleanser and detoxifier. In fact, it has been used to treat a wide range of conditions including eczema, measles, rheumatism, and gout. Its long, mucilaginous roots are edible and are highly prized in Japan, where cultivated burdock is called *gobo*. Its young stalks are also edible, either raw in salads or lightly boiled until tender.

OTHER NAMES: Beggar's buttons, great burdock
PLANT FAMILY: Asteraceae
HEIGHT: Up to 5ft
HABIT: Hardy biennial with ovate to heart-shaped green leaves and round purple flowers
HABITAT: Moist, neutral to alkaline soil in sun or light shade
USES: Culinary, medicinal

JACK-IN-THE-PULPIT ARISAEMA TRIPHYLLUM

OTHER NAMES: Indian turnip, bog onion
PLANT FAMILY: Araceae
HEIGHT: 6—12in
HABIT: Hardy perennial with blotched stalks and one or two leaves, made up of leaflets and a hooded striped, green to purple flower, consisting of a spathe curved over a spadix
HABITAT: Moist, well-drained soil in part shade
USES: Medicinal, culinary, decorative

This striking plant is native to eastern North America. The name "Jack-in-the-pulpit" is a reference to its distinctive, hooded flower, said to resemble a preacher in a pulpit. It is a plant to be treated with respect as it is poisonous when eaten fresh, containing calcium oxalate crystals which cause a powerful, unpleasant burning sensation in the mouth and throat and can also irritate the eyes if brought into contact with them. Despite this, Jack-in-the-pulpit can be eaten safely without adverse effects if dried properly or cooked thoroughly, and its tubers were a staple food of the Native Americans, who dried them and pounded them into a flour. The Native Americans also used it medicinally to treat ailments ranging from whooping cough to boils and snake bites. Its exotic appearance means that it is also valued as a border plant.

ARISTOLOCHIA BIRTHWORT

Native to Central and Southern Europe, birthwort grows wild in fields, meadows, and along roadsides. It has also been cultivated, as it has a long history of being used as an aid in childbirth, with records showing it in use for this purpose in Ancient Egypt. Its generic name is derived from the Greek *aristos*, meaning "best" and *lokhia* meaning "childbirth." Taken internally for gynaecological and obstetric disorders it promotes healing. It has always, however, had to be used with caution as it is also toxic and can trigger abortions. Applied externally it has been used to treat skin infections and wounds, particularly snake bites.

PLANT FAMILY: Aristoloceae
HEIGHT: 8—34in
HABIT: Hardy perennial with heart-shaped, green leaves and clusters of curved, tube-like yellow flowers
HABITAT: Well-drained soil in sun or partial shade
USES: Medicinal

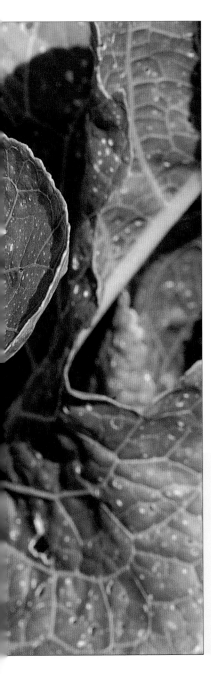

HORSERADISH

ARMORACIA RUSTICANA
(A. LAPATHIFOLIA, COCHLEARIA
ARMORACIA)

Native to eastern Europe and west Asia, horseradish is notoriously difficult to eradicate once established and consequently has naturalized throughout Europe and the USA. The plant has also long been cultivated for its leaves and its stout, white roots, both of which are edible. The English name "horseradish" derives from the word "hoarse" meaning coarse and strong and is a reference to its pungent odor and hot taste. During the Middle Ages, horseradish was used medicinally to aid digestion, as a diuretic and to treat urinary tract infections. In Europe the root also became popular as a condiment, mixed with vinegar and served with fish or meat. In Britain a relish made from grated horseradish is traditionally served with roast beef. Because the large, fresh root deteriorates quickly once sliced, it is traditionally preserved in vinegar or as a pickle.

PLANT FAMILY: Cruciferae
HEIGHT: 1—4ft
HABIT: Hardy perennial with long, green oblong leaves and tiny white flowers
HABITAT: Well-drained, rich soil in sun or partial shade
USES: Culinary, medicinal

ARNICA

ARNICA MONTANA

Native to Europe and west Asia, this pretty, aromatic herb is an alpine species, which grows wild in mountainous regions, thriving in cool conditions. Both its soft, downy leaves and its roots were smoked, leading to the nickname "mountain tobacco." For centuries, however, arnica has been best known for its healing properties in the treatment of bruises and sprains. It is also used to stimulate the immune system and the heart, with the German poet Goethe (1749–1832) reputed to have taken it for angina, and it remains a popular treatment for heart conditions in Germany today. Recent medical studies have questioned the safety of taking arnica internally. In homeopathic preparations, however, it is considered safe and is widely used.

OTHER NAMES: Mountain tobacco, sneezewort, mountain arnica
PLANT FAMILY: Asteraceae
HEIGHT: Up to 24in
HABIT: Hardy perennial with oval, hairy green leaves and orange-yellow, daisy-like flowers
HABITAT: Well-drained, humus-rich, sandy, acid soil in a sunny position
USES: Medicinal

SOUTHERNWOOD ARTEMISIA ABROTANUM

OTHER NAMES: Lad's love, old man
PLANT FAMILY: Asteraceae
HEIGHT: Up to 3ft
HABIT: Semi-evergreen, hardy shrub with branching shoots covered with feathery, gray-green leaves and clusters of tiny yellow flowers
HABITAT: Well-drained soil in sunny position
USES: Culinary, medicinal, decorative, insect repellent

Native to Southern Europe, this bushy shrub is nowadays primarily grown as a cultivated plant. Its strongly aromatic leaves repel moths and flies and it was a traditional component for nosegays. The French call it *garde-robe*, using it in their closets to protect their clothes. Medicinally, this bitter herb was used to improve digestion and liver function and also to stimulate menstruation. The seventeenth-century herbalist Nicholas Culpeper attributed to southernwood the power of curing baldness, recommending that a paste made from its ashes be rubbed on the head to promote hair growth. In the kitchen, its strong, bitter taste meant it was added sparingly, traditionally to flavor cakes and vinegars in France and Italy, and its leaves can be mixed into salads.

ARTEMISIA ABSINTHIUM WORMWOOD

Native to Europe and temperate Asia, wormwood grows naturally in waste places and on rocky hillsides. Since Egyptian times this notoriously bitter herb has been valued for its medicinal properties, considered to be a stimulating tonic. Its common name refers to its use in worming, and it was also used as a strewing herb and insect repellent. In the Bible the bitterness of wormwood is tellingly used as a metaphor for grim consequences: "But her end is bitter as wormwood" (Proverbs 5: 3–4). Essential oil of wormwood was a key ingredient in absinthe, an alcoholic apéritif invented in France in 1797. Addictive and fashionable, absinthe became notorious for its destructive effect upon those who drank it and was banned in 1915. Wormwood, however, is still added as a flavoring to liqueurs, tonic waters, and apéritifs.

OTHER NAME: Absinthe
PLANT FAMILY: Asteraceae
HEIGHT: Up to 3ft
HABIT: Semi-evergreen, hardy shrub with gray-green divided leaves and clusters of tiny, yellow flowers
HABITAT: Well-drained, neutral to alkaline soil in sunny position
USES: Medicinal, culinary

TARRAGON ARTEMISIA DRACUNCULUS

OTHER NAMES: Estragon, French tarragon, little dragon
PLANT FAMILY: Asteraceae
HEIGHT: Up to 3ft
HABIT: A bushy half-hardy perennial with long, slender green leaves and sprays of tiny yellow-gray flowers
HABITAT: Well-drained soil in a sunny position
USES: Culinary, medicinal

With its distinctive aromatic flavor, with faint liquorice overtones, French tarragon (as opposed to coarser-flavored Russian tarragon) is a popular culinary herb. It is particularly prized in French cuisine, where it is one of the *fines herbes* (a mixture of chopped fresh herbs). As well as to make tarragon vinegar it also lends its name to various dishes such as *oeufs en gelée à l'estragon*. It should be used fresh rather than dried, when its flavor is far more pronounced; and with discretion. Classically, tarragon is added to chicken, egg, and fish dishes, such as Béarnaise sauce. As well as being prized for its flavor, tarragon was thought to be an aid against flatulence. Its unusual Latin name (*dracunculus* meaning "little dragon") is thought to derive either from its twisted roots, which were thought to resemble a dragon, or from the ancient belief that it could heal snake bites.

ARTEMISIA VULGARIS MUGWORT

Native to the northern temperate zone, mugwort grows in waste ground or on waysides. There is a venerable history of using mugwort medicinally; it is mentioned in ancient Chinese medicinal lore and Greek and Roman writing, while the druids valued it as one of the nine herbs used to repel poison. Reputedly, Roman soldiers placed mugwort leaves in their sandals to help prevent tiredness on long marches. It was particularly known as a treatment for difficult or irregular menstruation and the menopause. Mugwort was known as the "mother of herbs" and has ancient associations with witchcraft and fertility rituals. In European cookery, mugwort's bitter flavor is used to cut through fatty foods, such as eel, goose, or duck.

PLANT FAMILY: Asteraceae
HEIGHT: 2—5½ft
HABIT: Hardy perennial with purplish stems and deeply cut, dark green leaves, and small, yellow or reddish-pink flowers
HABITAT: Well-drained, neutral soil in a sunny position
USES: Culinary, medicinal

DEADLY NIGHTSHADE

ATROPA BELLADONNA

Native to Europe, West Asia, and North Africa, this tall herb with its black berries grows in shady woods and hedgerows. Notorious as a poisonous plant, its generic name *Atropa* is thought to come from the Greek Atropos, the name of one of the Three Fates who cut the threads of life. Its common name "dwale" is from the Nordic *duale*, meaning something that causes stupor, a reference to the plant's narcotic properties. Historically, this deadly plant is reputed to have poisoned invading armies, famously used by Shakespeare's Macbeth against an invading Danish army. Despite this, deadly nightshade has also many useful medicinal qualities and was cultivated in medieval gardens. Squeezing the juice of the plant into the eye dilated the pupils, hence, apparently, the name "belladonna," which means "beautiful woman." Atropine, derived from the plant, is used in modern medicine as a narcotic, sedative, and diuretic.

OTHER NAME: Dwale
PLANT FAMILY: Solanaceae
HEIGHT: 3—5ft
HABIT: Hardy perennial with pointed, ovate, green leaves, and drooping, dark purple, bell-like flowers
HABITAT: Moisture-retentive alkaline soil in sun or partial shade
USES: Medicinal

DAISY

BELLIS PERENNIS

Native to Europe and Western Asia, the daisy is a very common grassland species, found in lawns and fields. It has long been regarded with affection for its appealing appearance, with its generic name *Bellis* meaning "pretty." The common name derives from the Old English "day's eye," referring to both the flower's appearance and the fact that it opens during daylight hours. In traditional medicine it was considered a wound herb, used to treat fresh wounds. Its other common name "bruisewort" refers to its use to relieve aches and bruises. In his *Herball* (1597) Gerard writes of daisies offering relief from the pain of gout when applied in a poultice to the joints. In the kitchen, its young leaves, flower buds, and petals may be added to salads.

OTHER NAME: Bruisewort
PLANT FAMILY: Asteraceae
HEIGHT: 1—6in
HABIT: Hardy perennial with rosettes of slightly toothed, oblong to ovate, green leaves and flowers consisting of a yellow disk surrounded by a fringe of several white or pink-flushed petals
HABITAT: Well-drained soil in sun or partial shade
USES: Culinary, medicinal

BORAGE

BORAGO OFFICINALIS

Native to the Mediterranean and Western Asia, this sturdy plant grows naturally on waste ground and has long been cultivated in kitchen gardens. Since ancient times, borage has been regarded as having a heartening effect, with Burton writing in his *Anatomy of Melancholy* (1621) of it as a good plant "to purge the veins of melancholy." Gerard, in his 1597 *Herball* writes of borage leaves and flowers being added to wine to "make men and women merry," a custom which continues today in Britain with borage flowers traditionally added to Pimm's, an alcoholic drink. Young borage leaves, with their mild cucumber flavor, can be used in salads, egg mayonnaise, or soft cheese dips while fresh borage tea is said to be useful against colds.

OTHER NAME: Starflower
PLANT FAMILY: Boraginaceae
HEIGHT: Up to 2ft
HABIT: Hardy annual with lanceolate, hairy, green leaves and five-petalled, star-shaped blue flowers
HABITAT: Chalky to rich, well-drained soil in full sun
USES: Culinary, medicinal

BOX BUXUS SEMPERVIRENS

OTHER NAME: Boxwood
PLANT FAMILY: Buxaceae
HEIGHT: 6—15ft
HABIT: Hardy evergreen shrub or small tree with gray-brown bark and glossy ovate leaves, and pale green, petal-less flowers
HABITAT: Well-drained, neutral to alkaline soil in sun or shade
USES: Medicinal, decorative, source of wood

Native to Europe, North Africa, and Turkey, this slow-growing, long-lived evergreen has long been cultivated. Its tough, close-grained, dense wood, twice as hard as oak, was highly in demand, used for printing blocks, cabinets, and mathematical and nautical instruments. For centuries, box has been used as a hedging plant, lending itself to topiary. Low-cut box hedges were a traditional component of classic, formal herb gardens. Box's essential oil was valued for its fever-lowering effects and in the treatment of epilepsy, syphilis, and malaria. Because of its toxicity, it was always used with caution and today its medicinal use is rare.

CALAMINTHA GRANDIFLORA CALAMINT

This hardy, aromatic plant is native to Europe, growing wild in hedgerows, woods, and along roadsides. In traditional medicine it was valued as an expectorant, while the seventeenth-century herbalist Culpeper recommended it for jaundice, nerves, convulsions, and "all afflictions of the brain." It was also known for causing abortions, containing as it does the active constituent pulegone. Its mint-scented leaves were traditionally used as a herb tea, made by steeping the fresh or dried leaves in boiling water, taken medicinally for weaknesses of the stomach or colic. Its ornamental appearance makes it an attractive addition to a herb garden.

OTHER NAME: Mint savory
PLANT FAMILY: Lamiaceae
HEIGHT: 15in
HABIT: Hardy perennial with square stems, toothed, ovate, green leaves, and pink-purple flowers
HABITAT: Well-drained to dry, neutral to alkaline soil in the sun
USES: Medicinal, decorative

MARIGOLD

CALENDULA OFFICINALIS

Native to Central Europe and the Mediterranean, the marigold is widely cultivated for medicinal, culinary, and ornamental purposes. Its generic name *Calendula* is derived from the Latin *Kalandae* the first day of the month in the Roman calendar. Long noted for its healing, antiseptic, and detoxifying properties, the marigold has a venerable history of medicinal use, dating back to early Indian and Arabic cultures and also Ancient Greece and Rome. In the Middle Ages, the marigold was used to treat a range of ailments, including intestinal problems, smallpox, and measles. Externally the plant was applied in the treatment of conjunctivitis, burns, and eczema. Marigold flowers, which contain the substance calendulin, are a traditional colorant, adding a yellow tint to cheese, butter, cakes, and rice dishes. It also has a history of use in cosmetics such as skin lotions.

OTHER NAME: Pot marigold
PLANT FAMILY: Asteraceae
HEIGHT: 20—28in
HABIT: Hardy annual with bright green, lanceolate leaves and yellow or orange flowers
HABITAT: Well-drained soil in full sun
USES: Culinary, medicinal, cosmetic, colorant

LADY'S SMOCK CARDAMINE PRATENSIS

OTHER NAMES: Cuckoo
flower, meadow cress
PLANT FAMILY: Brassicaceae
HEIGHT: 12—18in
HABIT: Hardy perennial
with a rosette of long-
stalked pinnate leaves
and small, white or lilac
four-petalled flowers
HABITAT: Moist soil in sun
or partial shade
USES: Culinary, medicinal

Native to Europe, North America, and North Asia, lady's
smock grows wild in damp grasslands. Its common
name "cuckoo flower" is thought to have come about
because the plant flowers at the same time as the cuckoo
arrives in Europe. Its generic name *Cardamine* derives
from the Greek *kardamon*, meaning "cress," as the plant
resembles watercress. It is traditionally thought of as a
tonic cleansing herb. High in vitamin C, its edible leaves
and flowers are traditionally eaten in salads. In Britain,
lady's smock is a plant with much folklore attached to it,
including the belief that it attracted adders. It was also
thought that picking the flowers resulted in lightning
and thunder.

CARTHAMUS TINCTORIUS SAFFLOWER

Native to West Asia, this thistle-like plant was introduced into Europe from Egypt and is today widely cultivated around the world. The name *Carthamus* comes from the Arabic *qurtom* or the Hebrew *qarthami*, which mean "to paint" and was given to the safflower because its flowers yield orange and red dyes. It has a long history of being used as a coloring for fabrics and foods, mentioned for this purpose in Egypt in 3000 BC; and as a red pigment for silk and rouge. In cookery it was seen as a cheaper substitute for saffron, hence its common names "false saffron" or "saffron thistle." Today, safflower oil, extracted from the seeds, is valued as a cooking oil, high in polyunsaturates, and the plant is grown commercially for this purpose.

OTHER NAMES: False saffron, saffron thistle, dyer's saffron
PLANT FAMILY: Asteraceae
HEIGHT: 12—24in
HABIT: Hardy annual with dark green, spiny, lance-olate leaves and yellow or orange, thistle-like flowerheads
HABITAT: Light, well-drained soil in the sun
USES: Culinary, colorant

CARAWAY

CARUM CARVI

Indigenous to West Asia and the Mediterranean region, caraway is found growing wild in grassy fields and waste ground. It is cultivated for its small, brown, aromatic seeds, high in carvone, which gives them their characteristic strong, aniseed-like flavor and scent. Caraway has a long history of usage in the Middle East and was also used by the Ancient Egyptians. Although medicinally caraway is a traditional treatment for indigestion, with its seeds chewed to freshen breath and aid digestion, it has primarily been used in the kitchen. Introduced into Europe in the Middle Ages, caraway plays a large part particularly in German and East European cuisine, adding its distinctive flavor to sauerkraut, rye bread, sausages, cheese, cakes, and liqueurs such as kummel; while in Victorian Britain, caraway seed cake was a popular tea-time treat.

PLANT FAMILY: Apiaceae (Umbelliferae)
HEIGHT: 2—3ft
HABIT: Hardy biennial with light green, feathery, fern-like leaves and clusters of tiny white or pinkish flowers
HABITAT: Well-drained or heavy soil in full sun
USES: Culinary, medicinal

CENTAURY CENTAURIUM ERYTHRAEA

OTHER NAMES: Bitterherb, feverwort
PLANT FAMILY: Gentianaceae
HEIGHT: Up to 10in
HABIT: Hardy biennial with basal rosette of wedge-shaped, green leaves and clusters of small, starlike, five-petalled, pink flowers
HABITAT: Well-drained, sandy soil, ideally in full sun
USES: Medicinal

Native to Europe and South-west Asia, centaury grows naturally on dry grassland, sand dunes, and cliff edges. Its common name "centaury" is said to have derived from the Greek mythological figure of the centaur Chiron, half man, half horse, famous for his knowledge of herbal medicine, who reputedly used the herb. In ancient times, centaury was seen as a herb possessing magical properties, thought to be a universal purifier. It has a long history of being used to stimulate the appetite and improve digestion. It is an extremely bitter herb, with the seventeenth-century herbalist Nicholas Culpeper writing of it "it is very wholesome but not very toothsome." Despite its off-putting taste, however, he recommended it for a variety of purposes, including killing worms, healing wounds, and against adder venom. It is still employed today as an appetite stimulant.

CHAMAEMELUM NOBILE CAMOMILE

This low-growing, creeping herb is native to Western Europe and North America, growing wild on verges and waste ground. The generic name "*Chamaemelum*" comes from the Greek *chamaimelon*, meaning "ground apple," after the apple-like scent the plant gives off when crushed. High in aromatic oils, camomile is little troubled by pests and indeed has been called a "physician plant" since it has a reputation for protecting sickly neighboring plants. During the Middle Ages this fragrant plant was a popular strewing herb for floors and there is a tradition of growing camomile lawns for their scent. Medicinally, camomile has long been a treatment for indigestion, with the dried flowers of both *Chamaemelum nobile* and *Chamomilla recutita* (German camomile) used in herb teas.

OTHER NAMES: Garden camomile, Roman camomile
PLANT FAMILY: Asteraceae
HEIGHT: Up to 1ft
HABIT: Hardy, perennial evergreen with finely divided, green leaves and long-stalked, solitary flowers with yellow disks and fine, white petals
HABITAT: Most soils, from full sun to light shade
USES: Medicinal, culinary, decorative

GOOD KING HENRY
CHENOPODIUM BONUS-HENRICUS

OTHER NAMES: All good, good King Harry, good neighbor, mercury, wild spinach

PLANT FAMILY: Chenopodiaceae

HEIGHT: Up to 24in

HABIT: Hardy perennial with large, arrow-shaped, green leaves and spikes of tiny, yellow-green flowers

HABITAT: Rich, well-drained soil in the sun

USES: Culinary, medicinal

Native to Europe, West Asia, and North America, this herb grows wild in pastures, verges, waste ground, and near ruins. Its generic name *Chenopodium* derives from the Greek *chen*, meaning goose, and *podus*, meaning "foot," a reference to its web-shaped leaves. Its unusual common name is thought to be after King Henry IV of Navarre. For centuries, the herb's young leaves have been eaten as a pot herb, while its young shoots were boiled and eaten as a poor man's asparagus. In traditional medicine its leaves were used to make poultices and also to heal sores, boils, and abscesses.

CHICORY
CICHORIUM INTYBUS

Native to Europe and West Asia, chicory grows wild in hedgerows, fields and on roadsides. Known to the Ancient Egyptians, Greeks, and Romans, chicory has long been an important herb, both medicinal and culinary. Medicinally it was used for purging, to treat sore eyes, as a remedy for gallstones, and as a digestive. Its bitter leaves were picked when young and tender and used in salads and cultivated chicory was developed from it in the sixteenth century. Bitter chicory roots have long been roasted to use as an adulterant to coffee. Its leaves were also boiled to produce a blue dye. There is much folklore attached to the herb, including the legend that its blue flowers are the eyes of a girl crying for her sweetheart lost at sea.

OTHER NAME: Wild succory
PLANT FAMILY: Asteraceae
HEIGHT: 3ft
HABIT: Hardy perennial with lance-shaped, toothed, mid-green leaves and purple-blue flowers
HABITAT: Light, alkaline soil in sunshine
USES: Culinary, medicinal, colorant

KAFFIR LIME

CITRUS HYSTRIX

Native to South-east Asia, the leaves and fruit of this citrus tree are widely used throughout the region. The Latin name *hystrix*, meaning "porcupine," is a reference to the tree's extremely sharp thorns. Its aromatic leaves are used fresh or dried to add a distinctive citrus flavor to a number of classic dishes, such as Thai green curries and tom yam soup. Dark green, Kaffir limes are easy to distinguish from other limes because of their distinctive knobbly skins. In Indonesia the lime is called *jerut obat*, meaning "medicine citrus" and the juice and rind of the lime are employed in traditional Indonesian medicine. Today, with Thai food increasingly popular in the West, Kaffir lime leaves are increasingly available in Europe, sold frozen, fresh, or dried.

OTHER NAME: Makrut lime
PLANT FAMILY: Rutaceae
HEIGHT: 10—15ft
HABIT: Small, evergreen tree with dark green, glossy, broadly ovate leaves with expanded petioles, and small white flowers
HABITAT: Well-drained, neutral to slightly acid soil
USES: Culinary, medicinal

WINTER PURSLANE
CLAYTONIA PERFOLIATA (MONTANA PERFOLIATA)

OTHER NAME: Miner's lettuce
PLANT FAMILY: Portulacaceae
HEIGHT: Up to 12in
HABIT: Hardy annual with perfoliate green leaves (that is, encircling the stem) and small, white or pinkish five-petalled flowers
HABITAT: Light, fairly rich, free-draining soil in full sun
USES: Culinary

Native to North America, winter purslane was introduced to Europe where it has since naturalized, and is found growing on dry soil along roadsides. The common name "miner's lettuce" can be traced back to the American Gold Rush in California, when prospectors ate the fresh, green leaves of the plant in spring to help them prevent scurvy after the shortages of harsh winters. Its blossoms and fleshy leaves can be eaten in salads or the leaves can be cooked and eaten as a green vegetable.

LILY-OF-THE-VALLEY
CONVALLARIA MAJALIS

Native to Europe and North America, the lily-of-the-valley grows wild in woodland and meadows and has been widely cultivated. Its generic name is derived from the Latin *convallium*, meaning "of the valley," and *majalis*, referring to May, the month in which this plant blooms. It is for its white, bell-like flowers, with their heady, fragrant scent, that the plant is best-known today and since the Middle Ages the flowers have symbolized modesty and purity. Historically, the plant was also valued for medicinal reasons, despite all parts of it being poisonous, it was used as a tonic for weak hearts. Today we know that the plant contains cardiac glycosides, which strengthen and regularize the heartbeat.

OTHER NAME: May lily
PLANT FAMILY: Convallariaceae
HEIGHT: 6in
HABIT: Hardy perennial with mid-green, long, oval leaves and stems of white, bell-shaped flowers
HABITAT: Moist soil in shade or semi-shade
USES: Medicinal, decorative

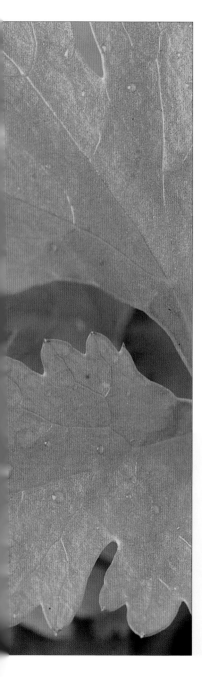

CORIANDER

CORIANDRUM SATIVUM

This aromatic annual, native to the eastern Mediterranean, is one of the oldest known herbs, cultivated for over 3000 years, used by the Ancient Egyptians and Romans and mentioned in Sanskrit texts. Its generic name is said to derive from the Greek *koriannon*, meaning "bed-bug," thought to be a reference to the plant's distinctive, pungent smell. Although the plant has a medicinal applications in the treatment of indigestion, it is as a culinary herb that coriander is widely used all over the world. In India its fragrant seeds are a fundamental spice, used to flavor curries and other dishes, while its leaves are an ingredient in fresh chutneys. In Latin America its leaves flavor fish, meat, and poultry dishes, while in Thailand the whole plant, including its roots, is used in curry pastes. In French cookery, coriander seeds are essential for dishes *à la Grecque* while in Germany it flavors sausages.

OTHER NAMES: Chinese parsley, cilantro
PLANT FAMILY: Apiaceae
HEIGHT: 6—28in
HABIT: Hardy annual with finely cut aromatic leaves and clusters of small, white flowers
HABITAT: Moderately rich, well-drained soil in full sun to light shade
USES: Culinary, medicinal

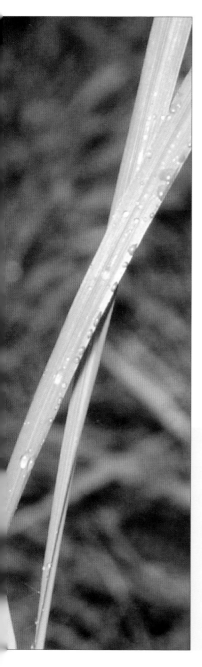

LEMON GRASS
CYMBOPOGON CITRATUS

Native to South-east Asia, this aromatic, tropical herb is today cultivated in many countries around the world. As its common name suggest, it has a distinctive lemon scent and flavor, due to its essential oil containing the constituent citral. Lemon grass is widely used in South-east Asian cuisine, adding its fragrance to numerous dishes including soups, curries, and sauces throughout the region. As lemon grass stalks are tough and fibrous, it is often simply crushed to release its aromatic oils and added whole. Alternatively, the outer casing is peeled off and only the lower, white, tender part of the stalk is finely chopped or crushed before using. When cooking with it, fresh lemon grass is infinitely preferable to dried. It is also valued as an insect repellent (usually under its other name "citronella") and used as a skin cleanser, a tonic, and an aid to digestion.

OTHER NAME: Citronella
PLANT FAMILY: Poaceae
HEIGHT: Up to 5ft
HABIT: Tender, clump-forming perennial with dense stems, and long, thin leaves
HABITAT: Well-drained soil in sun with moderate humidity
USES: Culinary, medicinal, cosmetic, insect repellent

CLOVE PINK

DIANTHUS CARYOPHYLLUS

Native to Southern Europe and North Africa, the clove pink is the wild ancestor of the cultivated carnation, now grown throughout the world. Its generic name *Dianthus* comes from the Greek *dios* meaning "god" and *anthos* meaning "flower." The clove pink's pretty flowers, with their strong clove fragrance, have long been valued both for their appearance and their perfume, used by the Ancient Greeks and Romans for garlands. It is one of the oldest flowers to be cultivated in Britain. In traditional medicine it was mixed in tonic cordials to treat fevers. Culinarily, its petals were used to flavor vinegars, ales, sauces, and salads, adding a spicy, clove-like taste. Candied petals (with the bitter white part removed) were a popular cake decoration, whilst dried clove pink petals are found in potpourris.

OTHER NAMES: Gillyflower, wild carnation
PLANT FAMILY: Caryophyllaceae
HEIGHT: 8—20in
HABIT: Hardy evergreen perennial with gray-green, lanceolate leaves and deep pink to purple flowers
HABITAT: Well-drained, neutral to alkaline soil
USES: Culinary, medicinal, decorative

DITTANY DICTAMNUS ALBUS

OTHER NAMES: Burning
bush, gas plant
PLANT FAMILY: Rutaceae
HEIGHT: 16—32in
HABIT: Hardy, clump-
forming perennial with
green, divided leaves
and loose pyramidal
spikes of white to pale
purple flowers
HABITAT: Well-drained,
neutral to alkaline soil in
sun or partial shade
USES: Medicinal,
decorative

Native to Europe, China, and Korea, this aromatic herb
grows in the wild in scrub and pine woods, but is also
cultivated. White dittany's common names, "burning
bush" and "gas plant," are a reference to the plant's
lemon-scented, volatile oils, which in calm, warm
weather form a vapor around it that can be ignited. There
is a long history of using white dittany medicinally, with a
description of it in Chinese medical texts from around
AD600. Its strong-smelling, bitter-tasting dried root bark
is employed in traditional Chinese medicine to lower
fevers and control bacterial infections, as an antispasmodic and to induce menstruation. It is little used
today in Western herbalism as, taken in large doses, it is
poisonous. Its attractive appearance and fragrant scent,
however, have made it a popular cultivated plant.

DIGITALIS PURPUREA FOXGLOVE

Native to Western and Central Europe and naturalized in North America, the common foxglove is found growing in woods and hedgerows. The generic name *Digitalis* is derived from the Latin *digitus*, meaning "finger." The foxglove's attractive and striking appearance, with its spires of bell-shaped flowers, has made it a popular garden plant, despite the fact that it is highly poisonous. In herbal medicine it was used to treat sores and wounds. In 1785, however, Dr Withering wrote of its efficacy as a treatment for heart problems, after analyzing a traditional herbal cure for dropsy that contained foxglove. Today, the foxglove is cultivated commercially for the pharmaceutical industry, with "digitalis" being the term for its powdered leaf used in tablets or capsules to treat heart failure.

OTHER NAMES: Dead men's bells, fairy's glove, purple foxglove

PLANT FAMILY: Scrophulariaceae

HEIGHT: 3—5ft

HABIT: Hardy biennial or short-lived perennial with large, hairy, ovate to lanceolate green leaves and a tall spire of purple, pale pink or white bell-shaped flowers

HABITAT: Well-drained, neutral to acid soil in partial shade

USES: Medicinal, decorative

SUNDEW DROSERA ROTUNDIFOLIA

OTHER NAME: Dewplant
PLANT FAMILY: Droseraceae
HEIGHT: 4—6in
HABIT: Hardy perennial with a rosette of red-green, sticky, spoon-shaped leaves and small, white five-petalled flowers
HABITAT: Wet peat in sun
USES: Medicinal, decorative

Native to temperate Eurasia and North America, this hardy perennial is found growing in peat bogs, marshes, heaths, and moors, often among sphagnum moss. It is insectivorous, secreting a digestive enzyme which attracts, catches, and dissolves insects. The generic name *Drosera* comes from the Greek *drosos*, meaning "dew," a reference to the droplets of enzyme on the plant's leaves. In traditional medicine the plant was used as a fortifying tonic and reputed to have aphrodisiac effects. Today, sundew is harvested from the wild for the plumbagin which it contains, active against a range of pathogenic bacteria. Sundew is also very popular with collectors of carnivorous plants.

ECHINACEA PURPUREA ECHINACEA

Native to North America, this attractive herb grows wild in woodlands but is today cultivated in a number of countries. The name "echinacea" comes from the Greek *echinos*, meaning "hedgehog," referring to its flower's prickly cone. Its medicinal properties were first discovered by Native Americans, who used a number of echinacea species to treat snake bites and infected wounds. During the 1930s a German herbal company imported the seeds of *Echinacea purpurea* to Europe. There has been considerable research into the herb and it has been discovered that echinacea stimulates the body's immune system. Today it is widely used as a herbal medicine, taken particularly to treat and prevent the common cold and influenza.

OTHER NAME: Purple coneflower
PLANT FAMILY: Asteraceae
HEIGHT: Up to 5ft
HABIT: Hardy perennial with large, hairy, ovate leaves and purple-pink, daisy-like flowers with orange central cones
HABITAT: Most soils in full sun or light shade
USES: Medicinal

VIPER'S BUGLOSS

ECHIUM VULGARE

Native to Europe, viper's bugloss grows on waste ground, uncultivated fields, and by roadsides and is now naturalized throughout the Northern Hemisphere, indeed considered an invasive weed by many. The generic name derives from the Greek *ekios*, meaning "viper," thought to be because its seeds resembled snakes' heads. Appropriately, this herb was indeed used to treat snake bites in medieval times. In the seventeenth century Nicholas Culpeper wrote of it: "It is a herb of the sun. It is an especial remedy against both poisonous bites and poisonous herbs." Its juice was also applied to smooth sensitive skin and treat boils. Its young leaves can be eaten in salads.

OTHER NAMES: Snakeflower, viper's grass
PLANT FAMILY: Boraginaceae
HEIGHT: 2—4ft
HABIT: Hardy biennial with mid-green, hairy, oblong to lanceolate leaves and funnel-shaped flowers that turn from pink to blue
HABITAT: Light, dry soil in full sun
USES: Culinary, medicinal

HORSETAIL EQUISETUM ARVENSE

OTHER NAMES: Bottle brush, mare's tail, shave grass

PLANT FAMILY: Equisetaceae

HEIGHT: 8—32in

HABIT: Hardy herbaceous perennial with long, brown-green, jointed stems and whorls of green branches

HABITAT: Moist soil in sun or partial shade

USES: Medicinal

Found from Europe to China and in North America, this striking-looking plant usually grows near water in fields, hedgerows, or waste ground. Remarkably it has survived barely changed since prehistoric times. It is a cryptogam, that is, a plant without flowers or seeds. Its striking, brush-like appearance is reflected both in its common names and its Latin name, which means "horse tail." The plant's unusual chemistry makes it able to absorb large amounts of silica from the soil and it was traditionally used to scour pots and pans because of its abrasive qualities. Since Roman times it has been used as a general tonic and an astringent and to stanch the flow of blood. The plant's high silica content means that it acts as a strengthener for fragile fingernails.

ERUCA VESICARIA SALAD ROCKET

Native to the Mediterranean, rocket is now widely cultivated in many countries, including North America. Its distinctive, peppery flavor means that it has been used as a salad herb since ancient times. The Romans prized it, considering it an aphrodisiac and eating both its tender leaves and its seeds. In French cuisine, rocket is one of the traditional leaves in *mesclun*, a salad from the south of France. Since the 1980s rocket has become increasingly popular in North America and Northern Europe. It is still traditionally eaten in salads, with the young leaves having a milder flavor than the older ones.

OTHER NAMES: Arugula, roquette
PLANT FAMILY: Brassicaceae
HEIGHT: 24—36in
HABIT: Hardy annual with lobed, toothed, green leaves and cream, four-petalled flowers
HABITAT: Moist, fertile soil in sun or partial shade
USES: Culinary

SEA HOLLY

ERYNGIUM MARITIMUM

Native to Europe, this striking, thistle-like plant grows naturally on sea shores. Its common name reflects both its natural habitat and its formidably prickly foliage. Historically, sea holly has had many uses. Its large, fleshy, mucilaginous, sweet-tasting roots have long been considered an aphrodisiac, sold in candied form as a popular sweetmeat. Its young shoots can be boiled and eaten. Medicinally, sea holly was used as an expectorant to treat coughs, and also a diuretic, easing bladder complaints. The seventeenth-century herbalist Nicholas Culpeper recommended it for easing "melancholy of the heart." Today it is often cultivated for its handsome appearance rather than for medicinal purposes.

OTHER NAME: Eryngo
PLANT FAMILY: Apiaceae
HEIGHT: 24in
HABIT: Hardy perennial with stiff, blue-green, lobed, spiny leaves and clusters of stalkless blue flowers
HABITAT: Well-drained, sandy or stony soil in the sun
USES: Medicinal, culinary, decorative

CALIFORNIA POPPY

ESCHSCHOLZIA CALIFORNICA

Native to western North America, this attractive plant grows in grassy, open areas and has naturalized in many other countries. A drought-tolerant, self-seeding herb, it thrives on disturbed land, often re-colonizing after fires. Its generic name is after the nineteenth-century doctor and naturalist Johann Friedrich Gustav von Eschscholtz. The California poppy was long used by Native Americans both as a food and as a medicine, eaten as a green vegetable and applied in the treatment of toothaches and to kill lice. It is a plant with mild sedative and analgesic properties and continues to be used for these, particularly for treating children.

PLANT FAMILY: Papaveraceae
HEIGHT: 3—4in
HABIT: Hardy annual with finely-cut, blue-green leaves and four-petalled, yellow to orange flowers
HABITAT: Well-drained to poor soil in full sun
USES: Medicinal, culinary

EUCALYPTUS

EUCALYPTUS GLOBULUS

Native to Australia, the eucalyptus is grown in other temperate countries to reclaim marshy land, as a windbreak, and for ornamental purposes. Its aromatic oil (high in cineole, which has the characteristic eucalyptus scent) has long been used medicinally. As it possesses expectorant and decongestant properties, it is made into inhalations and vapor rubs to treat bronchitis, catarrh, colds, influenza, and sinusitis. Eucalpytus is a traditional flavoring for lozenges, taken to ease coughing. Effective against many bacteria, it is applied externally in liniments to treat bruises, sprains and muscular pains, and in ointments for wounds and abscesses. Eucalyptus oil, however, must be used only as recommended, as large doses of the essential oil can cause headaches and convulsions and may prove fatal.

OTHER NAMES: Blue gum, Tasmanian blue gum
PLANT FAMILY: Myrtaceae
HEIGHT: Up to 150ft
HABIT: Tender tree with creamy white to gray bark that peels off in long, ribbonlike shreds and long, lanceolate, silvery blue leaves
HABITAT: Well-drained soil in sun
USES: Medicinal, decorative

JO PYE WEED EUPATORIUM PURPUREA

OTHER NAMES: Gravelroot, purple boneset
PLANT FAMILY: Asteraceae
HEIGHT: 4—10ft
HABIT: Hardy, clump-forming perennial with serrated, ovate, green leaves and clumps of small pink, purplish or white flowers
HABITAT: Moist soil in sun or partial shade
USES: Medicinal, decorative

Native to North America, Jo Pye weed grows wild in rich, swampy ground and damp ditches. Its common name is in honor of a Native American doctor from New England who used the plant to successfully treat typhus. The common name "boneset" comes about because of its use to treat bone-break or dengue fever in America. It was also used medicinally to treat kidney stones, urinary disorders, such as cystitis, and painful menstruation. Its numerous flowers attract butterflies, bees, and other insect pollinators and make it a popular plant for garden borders.

FILIPENDULA ULMARIA (SPIREA ULMARIA) MEADOWSWEET

Native to Europe and West Asia, meadowsweet grows wild in fens, marshes and meadows, and on river banks. The common name derives from the Anglo-Saxon term "meadwort," that is a herb (wort) used to flavor mead. It has a long history of use by mankind and is said to be sacred to the druids. Its highly scented, creamy-white flowers made it a popular strewing herb during the Middle Ages and it was also traditionally used in churches for weddings, hence the name bridewort. Medicinally it was given as a diuretic and to treat heartburn, gastritis, and peptic ulcers. Culinarily, meadowsweet adds a delicious fragrance to vinegar and herbal beers, and liqueurs.

OTHER NAMES: Bridewort, queen of the meadow
PLANT FAMILY: Rosaceae
HEIGHT: 2—4ft
HABIT: Hardy perennial with pinnate, toothed leaves, divided into pairs of leaflets and clusters of tiny, creamy-white flowers
HABITAT: Rich, moist to wet soil in sun or partial shade
USES: Culinary, medicinal, decorative

FENNEL

FOENICULUM VULGARE

Native to Southern Europe, wild fennel grows in wasteland and dry, sunny spots, particularly sea cliffs. It is an aromatic plant, with a distinctive anise-like flavor and scent, long used both medicinally and culinarily. Cultivated since ancient times, there are a number of varieties, with wild fennel noticeably bitter. In Greek mythology, Prometheus hid the fire he stole from the gods to bring to humanity in a hollow fennel stalk. The Romans ate fennel shoots as a vegetable and used the small, gray-brown seeds as a flavoring for sauces. Medicinally, fennel is noted as an aid to digestion, with fennel seeds prescribed for stomach pains, flatulence, and loss of appetite. Fennel tea is a traditional remedy for babies' colic. Fennel's height and graceful, feathery leaves make it a very attractive addition to garden borders or herb gardens.

OTHER NAME: Bitter fennel
PLANT FAMILY: Apiaceae
HEIGHT: 4—7ft
HABIT: Hardy to half-hardy biennial or perennial with bright green, feathery leaves and clusters of tiny yellow flowers
HABITAT: Well-drained, neutral to alkaline soil in full sun
USES: Culinary, medicinal, decorative

WILD STRAWBERRY

FRAGARIA VESCA

Native to Europe, West Asia, and North America, the wild strawberry grows in forests, clearings, and by roadsides. Since ancient times, it has been prized for its tiny but exquisitely flavored red fruit. Its generic name derives from the Latin *fragrans*, meaning "fragrant," a reference to its perfumed fruit. It has also long been used medicinally, taken to treat anemia, kidney and liver complaints, and gout. Wild strawberry leaf tea is said to be a good tonic. Strawberries were also used cosmetically, to combat wrinkles and soothe sunburn. Because of their low yield and fragile fruit, wild strawberries are not widely cultivated. The strawberries generally available commercially are descended from two American species, which bore larger fruit.

OTHER NAME: Wood strawberry
PLANT FAMILY: Rosaceae
HEIGHT: 10—12in
HABIT: Hardy, rosette-forming perennial with long runners and coarsely toothed, bright green, trifoliate leaves and four or five white-petalled flowers with yellow centers
HABITAT: Rich, neutral to alkaline soil in sun or partial shade
USES: Culinary, medicinal

FUMITORY FUMARIA OFFICINALIS

OTHER NAME: Earth smoke
PLANT FAMILY:
    Papaveraceae
HEIGHT: 12—16in
HABIT: Hardy, climbing or
    sprawling annual with
    silvery-gray, divided
    leaves and purple-
    tipped, pinkish-white
    flowers
HABITAT: Light, well-
    drained soil in the sun
USES: Medicinal

Native to Europe and Iran, fumitory grows in fields and wasteland, often clinging to old walls. Its generic name derives from the Latin *fumus*, meaning "smoke," but it is unclear why the association came about. One theory says there was a legend that it was born of the "vapors of the earth"; another that the plants' appearance from a distance was of a field on fire; while a third attributes it to the smoke it produces when burned. It has been valued as a purifying tonic since Roman times, particularly in the treatment of liver complaints. Taken internally and externally it is also used to treat skin complaints, such as eczema. If taken over too a long a period, however, the plant has sedative effects.

GALEGA OFFICINALIS GOAT'S RUE

Native to Europe, goat's rue grows wild by streams and ponds and is also widely cultivated. The herb's generic name *Galega* comes from the Greek *gala*, meaning "milk," because the plant was reputed to increase milk yield, a fact which has been borne out by scientific research. In traditional herbalism, goat's rue, which promotes sweating, treated fever, the plague, and snake bites. It has also been used to lower blood sugar levels and to treat diabetes.

OTHER NAME: French lilac
PLANT FAMILY: Papilionaceae
HEIGHT: 3—5ft
HABIT: Hardy perennial with pinnate leaves with six to eight pairs of bright green, lanceolate leaflets and lavender to white flowers
HABITAT: Moist, well-drained soil in sun or partial shade
USES: Medicinal

SWEET WOODRUFF GALIUM ODORATUM

OTHER NAME: Master of the wood
PLANT FAMILY: Rubiaceae
HEIGHT: 6in
HABIT: Hardy perennial with quadrangular stems, whorls of lanceolate, green leaves and star-shaped white flowers
HABITAT: Moist, well-drained, neutral to alkaline soil in shade
USES: Medicinal, culinary, insect repellent

Native to Europe, North Africa, and Russia, sweet woodruff, with its fragrant flowers, grows in shady woodland and hedgerows. Dried sweet woodruff has a delicious odor of hay, honey, and vanilla and was highly prized in medieval times as a strewing herb. It was also used to scent linen chests and ward off moths and in potpourri, snuffs, and perfumery. Medicinally, it has been employed in the treatment of menstrual pains and varicose veins, and as a sedative. In Germany, sweet woodruff is steeped in Rhine wine to create a delicately perfumed drink called *Maibowle*, drunk each year to celebrate May day.

GALIUM VERUM LADY'S BEDSTRAW

Native to Europe, West Asia, and North America, lady's bedstraw grows widely in the wild, found in wasteland, sandy grassland, and by roadsides. The generic name *Galium* derives from the Greek *gala*, meaning "milk," thought to refer to its traditional use to curdle milk in cheese-making, a quality made clear in its common name "cheese rennet." It was believed to promote sleep and used to stuff bedding, and in Christian legend was one of the herbs placed in baby Jesus's cradle in Bethlehem. Lady's bedstraw had numerous, traditional medicinal uses: as a diuretic, against epilepsy, and to treat skin complaints. The seventeenth-century herbalist Nicholas Culpeper believed it to be effective against nosebleeds. It was also employed in dyeing, with its roots giving a red dye popularly used for tartan in Scotland, and its stem and leaves a yellow color, popular with cheese-makers.

OTHER NAMES: Cheese rennet, yellow bedstraw
PLANT FAMILY: Rubiaceae
HEIGHT: 6—36in
HABIT: Hardy perennial with quadrangular stems, whorls of lanceolate, green, linear leaves and tiny, yellow flowers
HABITAT: Well-drained, neutral to alkaline soil in sun
USES: Culinary, medicinal, colorant

GARDENIA

GARDENIA AUGUSTA

Native to China, Japan, Taiwan, and
Vietnam, the gardenia is now widely
cultivated. The plant's generic name is in
honor of a noted botanist, Dr Alexander
Garden. The gardenia has a venerable
history of medicinal use in China,
mentioned in traditional medicinal texts
during the Han dynasty (AD25–220). It is
used to treat feverish colds and coughs, and
diabetes, to check bleeding, and also to aid
liver function. Taken externally it is applied
to wounds, sprains, and inflamed skin. Its
edible fruit is used as a coloring in Japan
and China, while its flowers flavor tea. In
the West, it is admired for its attractive,
fragrant blossoms and glossy foliage and
found in bouquets, wreaths, and corsages.

OTHER NAME: Cape jasmine
PLANT FAMILY: Rubiaceae
HEIGHT: 6—40ft
HABIT: Tender, evergreen shrub with glossy, dark green,
ovate to elliptic leaves and large, white flowers
HABITAT: Well-drained, humus-rich, sandy, neutral to
acid soil in light or partial shade
USES: Medicinal, decorative, colorant

WINTERGREEN GAULTHERIA PROCUMBENS

OTHER NAMES:
Chequerberry, creeping wintergreen, teaberry

PLANT FAMILY: Ericaceae

HEIGHT: 3—6in

HABIT: Hardy, evergreen, perennial shrub, with glossy, dark green ovate to elliptical leaves and drooping, white waxy flowers

HABITAT: Moist, peaty, neutral to acid soil in partial shade

USES: Medicinal, culinary

Native to North America and Canada, wintergreen is an aromatic, creeping, evergreen shrub which grows in the wild in cool, damp forests. It was long used by the Native Americans to treat aches and pains and to aid breathing. Oil of wintergreen, extracted from the plant, contains methyl salicylate, which gives the plant its distinctive medicinal scent. The oil has long had medicinal applications and has also been added as a flavoring for confectionery, cough drops, and toothpaste. Wintergreen tea, made from both the leathery leaves and from the berries, was a popular tonic while its red berries can be eaten raw or cooked in jams, jelly, or pies.

GENTIANA LUTEA YELLOW GENTIAN

Native to Central and Southern Europe, yellow gentian is found growing in pastures in mountains such as the Alps and the Apennines. The generic name is in honor of King Gentius of Illyria (c. 500 BC) who is said to have discovered the plant's medicinal uses. Its common name "bitterwort," meaning "bitter leaf," reflects the plant's intensely bitter taste. So bitter is it that it can be detected when diluted to 1 in 12,000 parts. For centuries the plant's roots have been used to make tonics, taken to treat loss of appetite, indigestion, liver complaints, and gastric infections. Today it flavors gentian liqueurs and Angostura bitters.

OTHER NAME: Bitterwort
PLANT FAMILY: Gentianaceae
HEIGHT: 3—6ft
HABIT: Hardy perennial with green, oval leaves and yellow, narrow-petalled flowers
HABITAT: Moist, light, well-drained neutral to acid soil in sun or partial shade
USES: Medicinal, culinary

LIQUORICE GLYCYRRHIZA GLABRA

OTHER NAMES: Sweet
  liquorice, sweetwood
PLANT FAMILY:
  Papilionaceae
HEIGHT: 5ft
HABIT: Hardy perennial
  with green, pinnate
  leaves with nine to
  twelve leaflets and pale
  blue to violet flowers
HABITAT: Rich, sandy soil
  in sun
USES: Culinary, medicinal

Native to the Mediterranean region, liquorice grows in
the wild in dry, open habitats but has long been widely
cultivated for its edible roots. Its generic name
Glycyrrhizia comes from the Greek for "sweet root" and
the plant's thick, long roots contain glycyrrhizin, an
intensely sweet substance. Known since Assyrian times,
liquorice was used medicinally by the Ancient Egyptians,
Greeks and Romans to treat coughs and colds. Small
pieces of liquorice root have long been sold as a natural
sweetmeat for chewing. Liquorice today is primarily
thought of as an ingredient in confectionery. In England,
liquorice cultivation is particularly associated with
Pontefract in Yorkshire, where the Dominican friars are
thought to have introduced it in the sixteenth century.

HAMAMELIS VIRGINIANA WITCH HAZEL

Native to the eastern states of North America, the deciduous shrub witch hazel grows in woodland but is also cultivated in America and Europe. The common name is thought to refer to the belief that the plant had magical powers, associated with witchcraft and with its forked twigs, used as divining rods. It has long been used medicinally by Native Americans who made ointments and infusions from its leaves and twigs to treat sprains, aching muscles, and bruises. It is an astringent herb that checks bleeding and reduces inflammation, and distilled witch hazel is widely used around the world to treat minor skin ailments. Its pretty, late-season flowers, with their fragrant scent, have made it an attractive plant for gardens.

OTHER NAMES: Snapping hazel, striped alder, winterbloom, American witch hazel

PLANT FAMILY: Hamamelidaceae

HEIGHT: 15ft

HABIT: Hardy shrub with broadly ovate green leaves, which turn yellow in the fall and clusters of two to four flowers with crinkled, yellow petals

HABITAT: Moist, humus-rich, neutral to acid soil in sun or partial shade

USES: Medicinal, decorative

CURRY PLANT

HELICHRYSUM ITALICUM (ANGUSTIFOLIUM)

Native to Southern Europe, the curry plant grows in dry, sunny places and is known primarily as a cultivated subshrub. Its silver-gray leaves give off a distinctive, spicy fragrance when brushed against, particularly after rain, hence its popular name. Its actual flavor is less strong than its scent, and it is used sparingly in cooking, with a few leaves being added to mayonnaise, cream cheese, and salads, or a sprig tucked into a roast chicken. With its scented, silvery foliage and yellow flowers, it is grown today mainly as an ornamental plant.

PLANT FAMILY: Asteraceae
HEIGHT: 24in
HABIT: Frost-hardy, evergreen subshrub with silver-gray, linear leaves and small, yellow, button-like flowers
HABITAT: Light, well-drained soil in sun
USES: Culinary, decorative

CHRISTMAS ROSE

HELLEBORUS NIGER

Native to Central and Southern Europe, the Christmas rose is found growing in woods in the wild, but is also cultivated as a popular garden plant. The word "hellebore," Greek in origin, came to mean plants that could cure madness. Christmas rose, its popular name, refers to its winter blooming. It has a long history of being used medicinally, with Pliny writing of it as a purgative in ancient times in the treatment of mania. The plant is, in fact, both an extreme purgative and toxic, able to cause abortions, so is little used today in herbal medicine. It is a herb with much folklore attached to it, associated with witchcraft and thought to be used by sorcerers to make themselves invisible.

OTHER NAME: Black hellebore
PLANT FAMILY: Ranunculaceae
HEIGHT: 2—8in
HABIT: Hardy, semi-evergreen perennial with dark green, leathery leaves and white or pink-flushed, five-petalled flowers
HABITAT: Moist, rich, neutral to alkaline soil in the shade
USES: Medicinal

HOPS

HUMULUS LUPULUS

Native to Europe, West Asia, and North America, hops grow wild in hedgerows and thickets but are widely cultivated. The common name is derived from the Anglo-Saxon *hoppan*, meaning "to climb," a reference to its climbing, twining habit. Hop shoots were eaten by the Romans as a vegetable and are still a popular vegetable in Belgium and France. Medicinally, hops were used for their sedative properties, as an aid to digestion and as a general tonic. Hops' best-known use, however, is as a flavoring for beer, a development which came about in Europe during the ninth century and gradually grew in popularity. There was much initial resistance to adulterating beer with this weed, but gradually its bitter taste and preserving qualities were appreciated. Today, it is also grown as a decorative climbing plant.

OTHER NAMES: Hopbind, hop vine
PLANT FAMILY: Cannabidaceae
HEIGHT: Up to 20ft
HABIT: Hardy, perennial climber with lobed, toothed, bright green leaves and conelike, pale green, female flowers, and clusters of tiny, green male flowers
HABITAT: Moist, well-drained, humus-rich soil in sun or partial shade
USES: Culinary, medicinal, decorative

HENBANE HYOSCYAMUS NIGER

OTHER NAMES: Hog bean, hen penny, stinking nightshade, black henbane

PLANT FAMILY: Solanaceae

HEIGHT: Up to 32in

HABIT: A hardy annual or biennial with pale green, ovate, hairy, lobed leaves and bell-shaped, purple-veined, creamy-veined flowers

HABITAT: Light, well-drained, neutral to alkaline soil in sun

USES: Medicinal

Native to Europe and West Asia, foul-smelling henbane grows wild on waste ground and roadsides in sandy or chalky soil. Its generic name derives from the Greek *hyos* and *cyomos*, meaning "bean of the hog." Its common name refers to the fact that its seeds are poisonous to poultry. It is, in fact, a toxic herb, to be handled with caution. Medicinally, however, it was used as a tranquillizer and to treat asthma, whooping cough, and motion sickness. It naturally had more sinister uses too, as a poison: in Shakespeare's play *Hamlet*, Hamlet's father is poisoned by having a distillation of henbane poured into his ear. In real life, Dr Crippen poisoned his wife in 1910 with an extract of henbane.

HYPERICUM PERFORATUM ST JOHN'S WORT

Native to Europe and West Asia, St John's wort grows wild in open woods, grassland, and waste ground. It is traditionally associated with St John the Baptist and has for centuries been highly regarded for its medicinal properties. Long used internally to treat nervous disorders and externally for healing, modern research has found it to contain the anti-depressants hypericin and hyperforin and to be a potent anti-viral. Today it is a popular herbal remedy, taken for the treatment of anxiety or mild depression and applied externally to bruises, burns, and wounds. It is used fresh or dried to make creams, infusions, liquid extracts, medicinal oils, and tinctures. Easy to cultivate, it is a picturesque addition to a herb garden.

OTHER NAMES: Grace of god, herb of St John
PLANT FAMILY: Guttiferae
HEIGHT: 2—3ft
HABIT: Hardy perennial with small, stalkless, ovate leaves and yellow, star-shaped, five-petalled flowers
HABITAT: Well-drained to dry soil in sun or partial shade
USES: Medicinal, decorative

HYSSOP HYSSOPUS OFFICINALIS

OTHER NAME: Blue hyssop
PLANT FAMILY: Lamiaceae
HEIGHT: 18—24in
HABIT: Hardy, semi-evergreen perennial with lance-shaped leaves arranged in whorls and spikes of tubular, blue, pink, purple or white flowers
HABITAT: Well-drained, neutral to alkaline soil in the sun
USES: Culinary, medicinal, cosmetic

Native to Europe, West Asia, and North Africa, this aromatic herb grows wild on dry, rocky slopes and walls. The generic name *Hyssopus* is derived from the Hebrew *ezob*, which means "holy herb." A herb called hyssop is mentioned in the Old Testament, used for purification, although there are doubts whether this was *Hyssopus officinalis*. In traditional medicine it was given to soothe chest complaints, coughs, and colds, with the seventeenth-century herbalist Nicholas Culpeper recommending it boiled with figs as a gargle. Its strongly aromatic, slightly bitter leaves and flowers were also added to salads, soups, casseroles, and sausages, though sparingly. It is the main flavoring of Chartreuse liqueur and is also used in making eau de cologne.

INULA HELENIUM ELECAMPANE

Native to Europe and West Asia, elecampane grows wild in fields and waste ground, but is usually cultivated. It has a long history of being used medicinally. Pliny wrote that the Roman Emperor Augustus declared "Let no day pass without eating some of the roots of enula [elecampane], considered to help digestion as well as mirth." Traditionally its thick roots were infused to soothe coughs, sore throats, and bronchitis, to aid digestion and as a general tonic. It was also used to treat skin complaints; hence its common name of "scabwort." Candied elecampane root was a popular medicinal sweetmeat from the Middle Ages to the twentieth century, taken for chest complaints and asthma. With its tall, erect stems and large, cheerful yellow flowers it is a popular addition to borders.

OTHER NAMES: Elf dock, horse-heal, scabwort

PLANT FAMILY: Asteraceae

HEIGHT: 10ft

HABIT: Hardy perennial with pointed, slightly toothed, green leaves and large, bright yellow flower heads

HABITAT: Moist, well-drained soil in sun

USES: Medicinal, decorative

ORRIS

IRIS GERMANICA VAR. FLORENTINA

Native to the Eastern Mediterranean, orris grows in the wild but is primarily a cultivated plant. The Greek word *iris*, meaning "rainbow," is possibly a reference to the plant family's varied colored flowers. Since ancient times, orris has been highly prized for its violet-scented roots, used in its dried form by the Ancient Egyptians, Greeks, and Romans for unguents and perfumes. Medicinally, despite being toxic if eaten, orris was a treatment for coughs and diarrhea. The iris flower is the origin of the *fleur-de-lys* and has been associated with the Italian city of Florence since the early Middle Ages. Today, the plant is cultivated in parks and gardens for its attractive appearance, while its root and essential oil are ingredients in cosmetics and sweets.

PLANT FAMILY: Iridaceae
HEIGHT: 2—4ft
HABIT: Hardy perennial with blade-shaped, green leaves and large, white, violet-tinged flowers
HABITAT: Well-drained, neutral to alkaline soil in sun
USES: Culinary, medicinal, cosmetic, decorative

JUNIPER

JUNIPERUS COMMUNIS

A conifer growing widely as either a shrub or small tree around the Northern Hemisphere, from the Mediterranean to North America, the juniper plant is valued for its aromatic berries. Probably their best-known use is as a flavoring for gin, the clear spirit-based drink first made by the Dutch in the sixteenth century. The Dutch name for juniper, "*jenever*," led to it being called "geneva," from which the English derived the name "gin." Long before its use in gin, juniper had been valued for its medicinal qualities, employed by both the Ancient Egyptians and Greeks and in Indian Ayurvedic medicine. Dutch geneva, in fact, first developed as a remedy for kidney disorders and today juniper is still used in herbal medicine.

PLANT FAMILY: Cupressaceae
HEIGHT: 1—25 ft
HABIT: Hardy evergreen perennial, with small, green, pointed needle-like leaves and small berries, dark blue-black when ripe
HABITAT: Chalky soil on heaths, moorlands, mountain slopes, and in coniferous forests
USES: Medicinal, culinary

WHITE DEADNETTLE LAMIUM ALBUM

OTHER NAME: Archangel
PLANT FAMILY: Lamiaceae
HEIGHT: 6—24in
HABIT: Hardy perennial
with ovate, coarsely
toothed, green leaves;
some species have
white stripe on leaf.
Tubular, two-lipped
white flowers
HABITAT: Moist, well-
drained soil in sun or
partial shade
USES: Culinary, medicinal

Native to Eurasia, the white deadnettle grows wild in
fields, hedgerows and waste ground, and along
roadsides. It is a creeping perennial which on first sight
resembles the stinging nettle (*Urtica dioica*), having very
similar leaves, but is actually not related botanically.
Medicinally it was used to check bleeding, so was
particularly associated with treating menstrual problems
and bleeding after childbirth. Able to reduce
inflammation, white deadnettle was also used as a
traditional compress. Its young leaves can be boiled as a
green vegetable or added to salads.

LAURUS NOBILIS BAY

Revered by both the Ancient Greeks and the Romans, the bay tree has an impressive and venerable history. Sacred to the Greek sun-god Apollo, patron of music and poetry, the bay was used to make the laurel wreaths that crowned emperors, generals, and athletes. This use is reflected in its Latin name, with *laurus* meaning "praise" and *nobilis* meaning "renowned." It has long been thought to protect against evil. In cooking, bay leaves are added fresh or dried and it is one of the herbs in a classic French *bouquets garni* (bundle of herbs). Bay leaves add their spicy flavor to a wide range of dishes, from stews and pasta sauces to pickled fish and marinated olives. Other historic uses of bay were as a strewing herb, to deter insects, and to treat indigestion.

OTHER NAMES: Bay laurel, sweet bay, sweet laurel
PLANT FAMILY: Lauraceae
HEIGHT: Up to 60ft
HABIT: An evergreen tree with smooth, glossy, dark green, pointed, oval leaves and tiny pale yellow flowers, followed by purple-black berries
HABITAT: Prefers full sun to moderate shade and tolerates most soils
USES: Culinary, medicinal

LAVENDER

LAVANDULA ANGUSTIFOLIA

Long appreciated for its fragrant, scented leaves and flowers, lavender is nowadays an extensively cultivated herb. Commercial growers in France produce it on a large scale for its essential oil, used to scent perfumes, soaps, and oils, and it is also a popular plant in yards, attracting bees and butterflies. The Ancient Greeks and Romans added lavender to their bathwater, both for its fragrance and for its therapeutic properties, hence its Latin name, from the Latin *lavare,* meaning "to wash." Thought to deter insects such as moths, lavender was employed as a strewing herb and to scent linen closets. Indeed, to this very day, small, pretty sachets of lavender are sold to scent wardrobes and drawers. In its infusion form, lavender has a sedative, calming effect and in aromatherapy lavender oil is a treatment for headaches and reducing tension. When it comes to the kitchen, lavender is not widely used, though sometimes it flavors sugar, syrups, and vinegar.

OTHER NAME: English lavender
PLANT FAMILY: Lamiaceae
HEIGHT: Up to 40in
HABIT: A hardy perennial with narrow gray-green leaves and spikes of purple flowers
HABITAT: Prefers full sun and well-drained soil
USES: Culinary, medicinal, cosmetic, insect repellent

CRESS LEPIDIUM SATIVUM

OTHER NAMES: Broad-
leafed cress
PLANT FAMILY: Brassicaceae
HEIGHT: 8—16in
HABIT: Hardy annual with
linear to pinnate, green
leaves and white, four-
petalled flowers
HABITAT: Well-drained soil
in sun or partial shade
USES: Culinary, medicinal

Native to West Asia, cress is widely cultivated for its
edible, peppery foliage. In Ayurvedic medicine, cress is
used to treat a range of conditions including indigestion,
coughs, asthma and, rheumatic pain. In the West,
however, it is regarded primarily as a culinary herb. A
fast-growing plant, cress is grown from seed and the
shoots are cut and eaten fresh at seedling stage. In
Britain, cress seed is classically mixed with mustard
seed to grow "mustard and cress," a traditional addition
to egg mayonnaise sandwiches. Its fresh leaves can also
be added to omelettes, salads, soups, and herb butters
and it is a traditional garnish.

LEVISTICUM OFFICINALE LOVAGE

Native to the Mediterranean, lovage grows wild in mountain pastures and by streams. In medieval times it was called *luvesche* and *loveach*, and it has a long tradition of being used in aphrodisiacs. It was a popular flavoring herb in Ancient Greece and Rome, mentioned by the Roman epicure Apicius, and continued to be widely grown in kitchen gardens during medieval times. Medicinally, its aromatic seeds were chewed to aid digestion. Infusions of the root were recommended for jaundice and urinary problems and its fragrant leaves were valued for their deodorizing and antiseptic properties. Today it is seen primarily as a culinary herb. Similar to celery, but with a milder flavor, lovage leaf-stalks and stem-bases can be blanched and eaten and its chopped leaves added to soups or salads or cooked as a green vegetable.

OTHER NAMES: Love parsley, sea parsley
PLANT FAMILY: Apiaceae
HEIGHT: 6ft
HABIT: Hardy perennial with green, divided leaves and tiny greenish-yellow flowers
HABITAT: Deep, rich, moist soil in sun or partial shade
USES: Culinary, medicinal

FLAX

LINUM USITATISSIMUM

Found in many countries throughout the world, flax is one of mankind's oldest cultivated crop plants, grown since 5000 BC. Flax seeds and linen woven from flax were found in Ancient Egyptian tombs, and in German mythology the gift of spinning and weaving flax was given to humans by a goddess. Since ancient times, flax seeds, high in linseed oil which has soothing and lubricating properties, were eaten medicinally. The Emperor Charlemagne decreed in the eighth-century that his subjects should consume flax seed for their health. Lin seeds and linseed oil are used to treat constipation and to relieve coughs, sore throats, tonsillitis, and colds. The crushed seeds are also a traditional poultice for burns, scalds, and ulcers. Culinarily, linseed seeds are baked in bread, sprouted for salads, or infused for tea. Research has shown that linseed oil is rich in essential fatty acids which may protect against heart attacks.

OTHER NAMES: Flaxseed, linseed
PLANT FAMILY: Linaceae
HEIGHT: 2½—4ft
HABIT: Hardy annual with narrow, gray-green leaves and blue, saucer-shaped flowers
HABITAT: Well-drained to dry sandy soil in sun
USES: Culinary, medicinal

HONEYSUCKLE

LONICERA PERICLYMENUM

Found throughout the Northern Hemisphere, honeysuckle in the wild grows in hedgerows and woodland but is also extensively cultivated. Its common name is said to derive from the custom of sucking the sweet nectar from its flowers. Its exquisite fragrance has long made it a prized plant and today there are many cultivars available to gardeners. Medicinally it was used as an expectorant, an antiseptic, and a diuretic. The sixteenth-century herbalist John Gerard mentioned the plant in his *Herball*, writing that its flowers steeped in oil were a good "anointment for cold bodies." Because of its heady perfume it has many associations with love and marriage. The scented flowers are used for potpourri, herb pillows, and cosmetics.

OTHER NAMES: Bindweed, woodbine
PLANT FAMILY: Caprifoliaceae
HEIGHT: Up to 30ft
HABIT: Hardy, deciduous perennial climber with paired, ovate, green leaves and yellow, trumpet-shaped flowers
HABITAT: Well-drained soil in sun or partial shade
USES: Medicinal, cosmetic, decorative

PURPLE LOOSESTRIFE LYTHRUM SALICARIA

PLANT FAMILY: Lythraceae
HEIGHT: 2—5ft
HABIT: Hardy perennial with lanceolate, green leaves and spikes of pink-purple flowers
HABITAT: Moist, neutral to alkaline soil or shallow water in sun or partial shade
USES: Medicinal

Native to Europe, Asia, and North Africa, purple loosestrife thrives in wetlands and marshy places. The generic name *Lythrum* comes from the Greek *lythron*, meaning "blood," thought to refer either to the blood-like color of the flowers or its beneficial effects on the body. It has a long history of being used medicinally, with the seventeenth-century herbalist Nicholas Culpeper recommending it particularly to treat eye infections. As purple loosestrife controls bleeding, it was used externally for wounds and sores and to treat internal bleeding, excessive menstrual flow, and nosebleeds. Scientific research has shown that it is effective against the bacteria that cause typhus and other feverish diseases.

MARRUBIUM VULGARE WHITE HOREHOUND

Native to Mediterranean Europe and Central Asia, aromatic white horehound is found in the wild in pastures and waste ground, and along roadsides. The generic name *Marrubium* may derive from the Hebrew *marrob*, meaning "bitter juice," as it is one of the five bitter herbs traditionally eaten during the Jewish festival of Passover. The plant contains a bitter principle, marrubin, a potent expectorant, and has been used as a cough remedy since Ancient Egyptian times. Candied horehound has long been a popular remedy for soothing coughs and sore throats. The plant is also known to have a sedative effect on the heart. Its culinary uses include flavoring herbal ales and liqueurs.

OTHER NAME: Common horehound
PLANT FAMILY: Lamiaceae
HEIGHT: 8—24in
HABIT: Hardy perennial with downy, gray-green, toothed leaves and stems and small, hairy off-white flowers
HABITAT: Well-drained to dry, neutral to alkaline soil in sun
USES: Culinary, medicinal

LEMON BALM

MELISSA OFFICINALIS

With its distinctive lemon scent when its leaves are rubbed, lemon balm is a fragrant and easy-to-grow addition to the yard. Beloved by bees, its generic name derives from the Greek *melissa,* meaning "honey bee." For centuries, lemon balm has been valued for various medicinal properties, with the Romans considering it a useful aid for reviving spirits. Brought over to Britain by the Romans, it was a popular herb in monastery gardens, used for refreshing teas and ointments. Its anti-melancholy associations have continued over the centuries, with the seventeenth-century diarist John Evelyn writing that "Balm is sovereign for the brain, strengthening the memory and powerfully chasing away melancholy." Today, it is used in aromatherapy to treat depression. Its culinary uses are in tisanes (with lemon balm and peppermint a popular combination), dressings, custard, fruit salads, and jellies.

Other names: Balm, melissa
Plant family: Lamiaceae
Height: 12—24 in
Habit: A hardy perennial with toothed, oval almost heart-shaped light green leaves and small, yellow-white flowers
Habitat: Prefers full sun or light shade in rich soil
Uses: Culinary, medicinal

PENNYROYAL MENTHA PULEGIUM

OTHER NAME: Pudding grass

PLANT FAMILY: Lamiaceae

HEIGHT: 4—8in

HABIT: Hardy perennial with elliptic to ovate, bright green leaves and small, purple flowers

HABITAT: Rich, moist soil in sun or partial shade

USES: Culinary, medicinal, insect repellent

Native to Europe and North Africa, pennyroyal is a creeper, cultivated particularly for aromatic ground cover and to deter ants, and so often grown between paving stones. As with other members of the mint family it is easy to grow and can be invasive. The name *pulegium* is derived from the Latin *pulex*, meaning "flea" because the plant's coarse, pungent scent was used to repel fleas and other pests such as mice. Its leaves can be rubbed on bare skin to act as an insect deterrent and medicinally, its oil can trigger abortions. The Elizabethan herbalist John Gerard recommended that its leaves be added to water on sea voyages to purify it. In England and Spain pennyroyal was a traditional flavoring for sausages.

MENTHA X PIPERITA PEPPERMINT

A cross between spearmint and water mint, peppermint has a pronounced aroma and flavor. The menthol in peppermint gives the herb its characteristic effect when eaten, that is, an initial hotness, followed by coolness in the mouth. This has made peppermint oil a popular ingredient in toothpastes, confectionery, such as chewing gum and mint sweets, and aftershaves. When it comes to cooking, peppermint oil rather than fresh peppermint leaves is used. Like other mints, peppermint is valued for its digestive and mouth-freshening qualities and peppermint sweets are often eaten after a meal. It is also considered to be an effective antispasmodic, a decongestant, and an antiseptic agent. As with other mints, peppermint is very easy to cultivate and should be grown in a pot to contain its invasive tendencies.

PLANT FAMILY: Lamiaceae
HEIGHT: Up to 3ft
HABIT: Hardy perennial with purple-tinged, dark green, lanceolate leaves and small pale purple flowers
HABITAT: Damp light soil in sun or partial shade
USES: Culinary, medicinal

SPEARMINT

MENTHA SPICATA

Spearmint, one of the best-known mints, has long been prized for its refreshing scent and flavor. In Greek mythology, Minthe was the name of a nymph transformed into the fragrant herb by the goddess of the Underworld. Introduced by the Romans to Britain, spearmint remains a popular herb to this very day. In British cookery it has a number of uses, adding flavor to new potatoes and peas or to make mint sauce or jelly, a classic accompaniment for roast lamb. A hardy plant, it is very easy to grow; indeed, it can become an invasive nuisance if not contained in a pot. Spearmint was historically valued for its digestive and mouth-freshening qualities and mint tea is served after meals throughout the Middle East. During the Middle Ages it was used as a strewing herb and to deter rats and mice from grain stores.

OTHER NAME: Garden mint
PLANT FAMILY: Lamiaceae
HEIGHT: Up to 3ft
HABIT: Hardy perennial with spearhead-shaped leaves and sprigs of tiny pale purple, pink or white flowers
HABITAT: Damp, light soil in sun or partial shade
USES: Culinary, medicinal, repellent

BERGAMOT

MONARDA DIDYMA

Native to North America, this attractive, flowering perennial grows wild in woodlands and by streams and is also a popular cultivated, ornamental plant. The common name "bergamot" is in tribute to its scent, similar to that of bergamot orange, while "bee balm" is thought to refer to the plant's appeal to bees and other pollinating insects, drawn by its fragrant, nectar-rich flowers. The plant's medicinal properties were well known by Native American tribes, who extracted and inhaled its oil to soothe bronchial complaints. They also made bergamot tea, known as Oswego tea after the Oswego Indians, and this became popular with colonists, especially after the Boston Tea Party when Indian tea was boycotted. Culinarily, its leaves and flowers can be used sparingly in salads, stuffings, lemonade and sauces.

OTHER NAMES: Bee balm, oswego tea
PLANT FAMILY: Lamiaceae
HEIGHT: 16—48in
HABIT: Hardy perennial with dark green, ovate to lanceolate, coarsely toothed, rough-textured leaves and bright red, claw-shaped flowers
HABITAT: Rich, moist soil in sun
USES: Culinary, medicinal, decorative

CURRY LEAF

MURRAYA KOENIGII

Native to India, Bangladesh and Sri Lanka, the curry tree is now widely cultivated in tropical countries. The name "curry" (from the Tamil word "*kari,*" meaning "spicy sauce") is a reference to the leaves' strong spicy smell and flavor. It has long been valued in South Asia as both a medicinal and culinary herb. In South Asian traditional medicine it was used to treat the digestive system, skin conditions, and diabetes, with modern research proving that it does indeed have anti-diabetic properties. Tamil literature from the first to fourth centuries AD mentions the aromatic leaf as a flavoring for vegetables and it is widely used in Asian cuisine. Traditionally, fresh leaves are added whole to dishes such as curries or dhals, in the same way that bay leaves are used to infuse dishes in Italian cookery. It is widely cultivated commercially and is also a popular ornamental plant.

OTHER NAME: Indian bay
PLANT FAMILY: Rutaceae
HEIGHT: 20ft
HABIT: Tender, evergreen tree with dark gray bark, pinnate, green leaves, and small white flowers
HABITAT: Moist, humus-rich, well-drained soil in sun or partial shade
USES: Culinary, medicinal, decorative

SWEET CICELY MYRRHIS ODORATA

OTHER NAMES: Garden myrrh, sweet bracken, sweet chervil
PLANT FAMILY: Apiaceae
HEIGHT: 3—6ft
HABIT: Hardy perennial with fern-like leaves and clusters of tiny white flowers
HABITAT: Moist, humus-rich soil in sun or shade
USES: Culinary, medicinal, decorative

Native to Europe, sweet cicely grows wild in meadows, woods, and hedges. The specific name *odorata* comes from the Latin *odorus*, meaning "fragrant," a reference to the plant's perfume. It has been cultivated for centuries, for both culinary and medicinal purposes. The sixteenth-century herbalist John Gerard recommended sweet cicely for treating coughs, consumption, digestive upsets, and as a tonic. The roots can be used as a vegetable, either cooked or raw in salads. Its leaves, with their delicate, sweet, anise-like flavor, are traditionally added to *bouquets garnis*, soups, stews, or salads and to fruit and cream as a fragrant sweetener. Its seeds, too, can be added to fruit salads or fruit pies. With its dainty leaves and flowers it is an attractive addition to a herb garden.

MYRTUS COMMUNIS MYRTLE

Native to the Mediterranean and South-west Europe, this fragrant, flowering shrub can be found growing wild in scrubland but is more usually cultivated. In Ancient Greece, myrtle was considered sacred to Aphrodite, the goddess of love, and traditionally planted near her temples. It is, therefore, used in wedding bouquets in the Middle East. Medicinally, myrtle leaf tea was a soothing expectorant and research has shown that it possesses antibiotic properties. Myrtle berries were eaten in ancient times as a breath-sweetener. Its leaves, flower buds, and berries add flavor to hams, sauces, and meat dishes, particularly in the islands of Corsica and Sardinia.

PLANT FAMILY: Myrtaceae
HEIGHT: 10ft
HABIT: Half-hardy, evergreen, perennial shrub with glossy, dark green, oval leaves and white flowers with golden stamens
HABITAT: Well-drained, neutral to alkaline soil in sun
USES: Culinary, medicinal, decorative

WATERCRESS
NASTURTIUM OFFICINALE
(RORIPPA NASTURTIUM-AQUATICUM)

Native to Europe and Asia, watercress grows in the wild in shallow water in streams, rivers, and ditches and is also widely cultivated. The generic name is derived from the Latin *nasus tortus*, meaning "twisted nose," a reference to the plant's pungent smell. Since ancient times its pleasantly sharp, peppery leaves have been eaten not only for their flavor but for their health-giving properties. The Greek general Xenophon prescribed it to his soldiers as a tonic, while the Ancient Greek physician Hippocrates recommended it as an expectorant and stimulant. Indeed, watercress is rich in vitamins A and C, iron and other minerals. Today, it is primarily used as a culinary herb, fresh or cooked in salads, soups, and stir-fries and as a garnish, particularly for meat and poultry dishes.

PLANT FAMILY: Brassicaceae
HEIGHT: 4—26in
HABIT: Aquatic, hardy, evergreen perennial with glossy, dark-green, pinnate leaves divided into three to five pairs of ovate leaflets and tiny, four-petalled white flowers
HABITAT: Shallow, flowing, slightly alkaline water in sun
USES: Culinary, medicinal

CATNIP

NEPETA CATARIA

Native to Europe and East and West Asia, catnip grows in the wild near streams and on roadsides. Its common names "catnip" and "catmint" refer to the plant's well-known effect on felines, who nibble the leaves and roll upon the plant with obvious pleasure. It is thought that the main component of the plant's volatile oil, nepetalactone, resembles a feline sexual pheromone. Despite its enlivening effect on cats, catnip was employed in traditional herbal medicine as a sedative, drunk in infusion form to calm nerves and to treat insomnia, stomach upsets, and colds and influenza. Its leaves can be used to make a mint-flavored tea and added to salads, sauces, and stews. Commercially, the herb's best-known use is in catnip toys for felines.

OTHER NAME: Catmint
PLANT FAMILY: Lamiaceae
HEIGHT: 1—5ft
HABIT: Hardy perennial with gray-green, ovate, toothed leaves and small whitish or pinkish flowers
HABITAT: Moist, well-drained soil in sun
USES: Culinary, medicinal

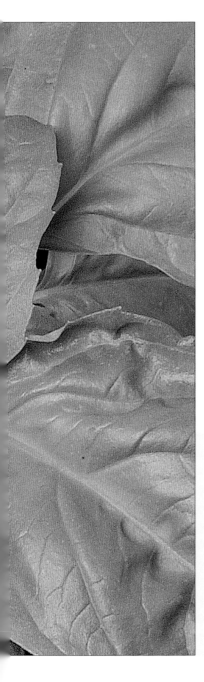

BASIL

OCIMUM BASILICUM

Thought to be native to India and the Middle East, basil is now cultivated around the world, with many varieties available. There are a number of ancient beliefs and myths associated with basil; it was said to have grown round Christ's tomb after the Resurrection and was seen as a symbol of love. It also had a darker side, thought to breed scorpions and associated by the Ancient Greeks and Romans with poverty and misfortune. In culinary terms, basil is particularly linked with Mediterranean cuisine, where it adds its aroma to dishes such as tomato salads, pasta sauces, and soups. Most famously, it is the key ingredient in pesto, a blend of basil, garlic, pine nuts, Parmesan cheese, and olive oil originating from the Italian port of Genoa, hence the name "Genovese." Historic medicinal applications range from a digestive aid to a cough mixture.

OTHER NAMES: Sweet basil, Genovese
PLANT FAMILY: Lamiaceae
HEIGHT: Up to 20in
HABIT: A bushy annual with oval, bright green leaves and spires of tiny white flowers
HABITAT: Prefers full sun with fairly rich, free-draining soil
USES: Culinary, medicinal

EVENING PRIMROSE Oenothera Biennis

OTHER NAMES: Fever plant, night willowherb, tree primrose

PLANT FAMILY: Onagraceae

HEIGHT: 3—5ft

HABIT: Hardy biennial with long, green, oval or lanceolate leaves and large, bowl-shaped, yellow flowers

HABITAT: Well-drained to dry soil in sun

USES: Medicinal

Native to North America, the evening primrose grows wild on steep banks, dunes, waste ground, and in fields and is also cultivated. The common name refers to its habit of opening its fragrant, yellow flowers in the early evening. The Native Americans have long valued the plant for its medicinal properties, using it in poultices to treat skin problems and bruises. Today it is a widely used herb supplement, taken particularly to treat pre-menstrual tension and applied externally to treat eczema. It is also taken to prevent rheumatoid arthritis and ease depression. Research has shown the plant to be high in an oil containing the essential fatty gamma-linolenic acid and there is much pharmaceutical interest in its medical potential.

ORIGANUM MAJORANA SWEET MARJORAM

Native to Southern Europe, North Africa, and Turkey, sweet marjoram grows in the wild in sunny, sheltered spots but is also cultivated for its aromatic leaves. Its popular name of "knotted marjoram" is thought to be a reference to its small, round flower buds, resembling knots on stems. Medicinally, it is a relaxing, warming herb, taken internally for bronchial complaints, headaches, and insomnia. It is as a culinary herb, however, that it is primarily known. Its leaves and flowers, with their delicate scent and sweet, aromatic flavoring, are used fresh and dried in sausages, herb scones, salads, omelettes, and sauces as well as in *bouquets garnis*. Dried sweet marjoram is also popular for potpourri.

OTHER NAMES: Knot marjoram, knotted marjoram

PLANT FAMILY: Lamiaceae

HEIGHT: 24in

HABIT: Half-hardy perennial with downy, gray-green ovate leaves and clusters of small white to pink flowers

HABITAT: Well-drained, average to rich soil in sun

USES: Culinary, medicinal

OREGANO

ORIGANUM VULGARE

Native to Europe, oregano favours dry, chalky soil, growing on hillsides in dry pastures and along hedgebanks. The generic name is from the Greek *oros*, meaning "mountain," and *ganos*, meaning "joy." Medicinally, the Ancient Greeks used it as an antidote to poison, as a disinfectant, and a preservative. Today, this aromatic herb, with its pungent flavor, is primarily used in the kitchen. It is particularly associated with Mediterranean cookery, adding flavor in its dried form to dishes such as Italian tomato sauces for pizzas or hearty Greek stews. Its oil is used commercially in toiletries and perfumes.

OTHER NAME: Wild marjoram
PLANT FAMILY: Lamiaceae
HEIGHT: 12—36in
HABIT: Hardy perennial with ovate green leaves on purplish stems and clusters of pinkish purple flowers
HABITAT: Well-drained to dry, neutral to alkaline soil in sun
USES: Culinary, medicinal, cosmetic

OPIUM POPPY
PAPAVER SOMNIFERUM

OTHER NAME: White poppy
PLANT FAMILY:
Papaveraceae
HEIGHT: 1—5ft
HABIT: Hardy annual with
gray-green, deeply
toothed leaves and
large, white to pink to
purplish flowers
HABITAT: Well-drained soil
in sun
USES: Culinary, medicinal

Native to the Mediterranean and Western Asia, but now
naturalized in many countries the opium poppy is also
cultivated. Its specific name *somniferum* is derived from
the Latin for "sleep-bringing," a reference to its notable
narcotic qualities. It has been used as a sedative for many
centuries, known to the Ancient Egyptians, Sumerians,
and Ancient Greeks. It is the plant from which both
opium and morphine are derived and as such its
cultivation is legally restricted in many countries. Poppy
seeds, however, contain no drug and are used in breads
and pastries or to thicken dishes such as curries. Its
cold-pressed oil is used for salad dressings.

ROSE-SCENTED GERANIUM
PELARGONIUM CAPITATUM

Native to South Africa, this low, spreading perennial is now widely grown as a decorative plant. It is actually a pelargonium, not to be confused with the geranium despite its misleading common name and similar appearance. Scented-leafed pelargoniums were introduced to Europe in the seventeenth century, and have been cultivated since, valued for their fragrant leaves and pretty flowers. In South Africa the plant was traditionally used medicinally to treat kidney and digestive disorders. Its perfumed, rose-scented oil is found in geranium oil, used in aromatherapy, perfumery, and cosmetic products.

OTHER NAME: Wild rose geranium

PLANT FAMILY: Geraniaceae

HEIGHT: 12—36in

HABIT: Tender perennial with velvety, crinkly, three to five lobed leaves and clusters of pink to pale purple flowers

HABITAT: Well-drained, neutral to alkaline soil

USES: Medicinal, cosmetic, decorative

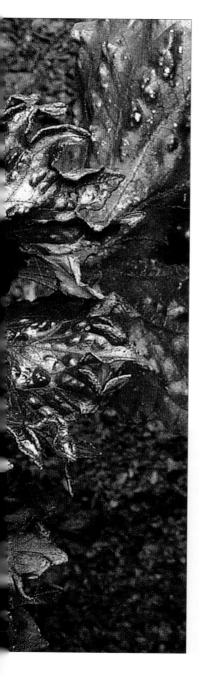

SHISO

PERILLA FRUTESCENS
(PERILLA OCIMODES)

Found from the Himalayas to Japan, shiso is widely grown in East Asia, valued particularly for its pungent, aromatic leaves. Its history of medicinal use in China dates back to around 500AD, where its stems are a traditional remedy for morning sickness. It is used to treat a wide range of ailments, including colds, coughs, constipation, food poisoning, and allergic reactions to seafood. As a culinary herb it is especially popular in Japan, used when fresh as a garnish in salads and when pickled as a condiment. The plant's "red" (actually purple) leaves are famous as a coloring and flavoring agent for Japanese pickled plums (*omeboshi*). The plant's seeds are also roasted and crushed for their edible oil, high in polyunsaturates.

OTHER NAMES: Beefsteak plant, perilla
PLANT FAMILY: Lamiaceae
HEIGHT: 2—4ft
HABIT: Hardy annual with ovate, pointed, toothed, green, sometimes purple-flecked leaves and spikes of tiny white to pink flowers
HABITAT: Well-drained, moist, fertile soil in sun or partial shade
USES: Culinary, medicinal

PARSLEY

PETROSELINUM CRISPUM

Today, this most familiar of herbs is taken for granted, perhaps because of its ubiquitous use as a garnish. In fact, parsley has long been a valued medicinal herb, credited by the herbalist Culpeper with treating many diseases, including liver and kidney complaints. There are many beliefs and superstitions associated with it; the Ancient Greeks decorated tombs with parsley and the Ancient Romans wore parsley wreaths at banquets to prevent intoxication. Its long germination time (seventy to ninety days) led to the old saying that parsley seed goes six times to the Devil and back before germinating. With its distinctive yet subtle fresh flavor, parsley is a widely used culinary herb. It is a key ingredient in French *bouquets garnis*, sauces (including parsley sauce), stock, and herb butters. Its high chlorophyll content makes it a useful breath freshener and it's also a good source of vitamins C and A and iron.

OTHER NAME: Curly parsley
PLANT FAMILY: Apiaceae
HEIGHT: 12—16in
HABIT: A hardy biennial with dense heads of small, bright green, curly toothed leaves and flat-topped clusters of creamy white flowers
HABITAT: Prefers full sun or light shade and fertile, well-drained soil
USES: Culinary, medicinal

FLAT-LEAFED PARSLEY

PETROSELINUM CRISPUM VAR. NEAPOLITANUM/FRENCH

There are two main varieties of parsley: curly and flat-leafed. Flat-leafed parsley has a stronger flavor than curly-leafed parsley and this is the parsley generally used for culinary purposes on mainland Europe and in the Middle East. Medicinally, parsley has been used in various ways since ancient times. Its diuretic properties mean it was a traditional treatment for urinary infections and gout. Flat-leafed parsley adds a characteristic fresh flavor to a number of dishes, most famously the Middle Eastern salad tabbouleh, consisting of generous amounts of finely chopped flat-leafed parsley, bulgur wheat, tomato, and spring onion.

OTHER NAMES: Broad-leafed parsley, French parsley, Italian parsley
PLANT FAMILY: Apiaceae
HEIGHT: 18—24in
HABIT: A hardy biennial with flat, dark green, segmented leaves and flat-topped clusters of small, creamy white flowers
HABITAT: Fertile, well-drained soil, full-sun or light shade
USES: Culinary, medicinal

SOLOMON'S SEAL POLYGONATUM ODORATUM

PLANT FAMILY:
Convallariaceae
HEIGHT: 34in
HABIT: Hardy perennial
with ovate, pointed
green leaves and
white, waxy, green-
tipped flowers
HABITAT: Well-drained,
rich, moist soil in
partial shade
USES: Medicinal,
decorative

Native to Europe and Asia, Solomon's seal grows in woods and shrublands. There are various theories as to the origins of its striking name. One theory is that Solomon set his seal upon its roots (which resemble broken Hebrew characters) in recognition of its medicinal value. Another suggestion is that the name came about because the plant could seal wounds. Solomon's seal certainly has a long history of medicinal use, known in classical times and in China during the first century AD. In Chinese medicine its rhizomes are used to treat dry coughs, heart disease, and tuberculosis. In Ayurvedic medicine it is seen as an aphrodisiac and a treatment for infertility. The sixteenth-century herbalist Gerard recommended using it either in poultice form or as a herb ale to glue together broken bones. Today in Europe it is primarily grown as an ornamental plant.

PORTULACA OLERACEA PURSLANE

Thought to originate from India, purslane grows wild in fields and by roadsides. It has been long been cultivated as a salad and pot herb, known to the Ancient Egyptians and grown in India and China for thousands of years. Medicinally, it is a diuretic, cooling herb, used to lower fevers, clear toxins, and treat bacterial infections. In Egypt it is a traditional remedy for sore eyes and skin inflammation. Research has shown purslane to be high in omega-3 fatty acids, thought to strengthen the immune system. Its mild-tasting fresh leaves can be eaten in salads, such as the Middle Eastern fattoush, or cooked as a vegetable, whereupon they take on a mucilaginous texture.

PLANT FAMILY: Portulacaceae

HEIGHT: 8—18in

HABIT: Half hardy, trailing annual with fleshy, rounded, bright green leaves and small, four to six petalled, yellow flowers

HABITAT: Rich, moist, well-drained soil in sun

USES: Culinary, medicinal

CINQUEFOIL

POTENTILLA ERECTA

Native to Northern Europe and West Asia, cinquefoil grows in grassland and on heaths and mountain meadows. The generic name *Potentilla* derives from the Latin *potens*, meaning "powerful," a reference to its curative properties. In traditional medicine, cinquefoil is valued as a strong astringent, taken internally to treat diarrhea and inflammation of the colon. Externally, decoctions of cinquefoil are used to treat piles, ulcers, cuts, sores and burns, and as a wash for sore eyes. High in tannin and a red coloring agent, its root was also traditionally employed to tan leather and to dye it red.

OTHER NAMES: Bloodroot, tormentil, shepherd's knot
PLANT FAMILY: Rosaceae
HEIGHT: 8—12in
HABIT: Hardy perennial with three-lobed, toothed, green leaves and four-petalled, yellow flowers
HABITAT: Light, acid soil in sun or light shade
USES: Medicinal, colorant

COWSLIP

PRIMULA VERIS

Native to Northern and Central Europe, the cowslip grows in the wild in fields and roadside verges in chalky and limestone areas. Its generic name *Primula* derives from the Latin *primus*, meaning "first," referring to its early flowering in the spring. Less poetically, its common name "cowslip" is said to derive from Old English *cuslyppe*, meaning "cowpat." Its other common names refer to the flower head's resemblance to the bunch of keys that St. Peter carries. Medicinally, cowslip wine and cowslip tea are valued for their calming, sedative qualities, and the herb was used to treat spasms, cramps, and paralytic ailments. Its flowers can be eaten fresh in salads or candied and used as decoration. It should not be collected from the wild, however, as it is nowadays a rare plant. Cultivated cowslips, however, are popular with gardeners.

OTHER NAMES: Herb Peter, key flower, keys of heaven, paigle
PLANT FAMILY: Primulaceae
HEIGHT: 6—8in
HABIT: Hardy perennial with rough-textured, oblong, green leaves and clusters of small, tubular, yellow flowers
HABITAT: Dry, neutral to alkaline soil in sun or partial shade
USES: Culinary, medicinal, decorative

PRIMROSE PRIMULA VULGARIS

PLANT FAMILY: Primulaceae
HEIGHT: 6in
HABIT: Hardy perennial with wrinkled green, oblong leaves and pale yellow flowers with notched petals
HABITAT: Moist, well-drained soil in sun or shade
USES: Culinary, medicinal, decorative

Native to Europe and North-Asia, the primrose grows wild in woods, hedgerows, and fields and is also cultivated. Traditionally it was seen as a medicinal plant, recommended by the Roman natural historian Pliny for rheumatism, gout, and paralysis. The seventeenth-century herbalist Nicholas Culpeper advised using it for healing wounds. Its roots were used to treat headaches and in fact the plant does contain salicylates, as in aspirin. It was also a traditional expectorant, employed in the treatment of bronchitis. Today, however, it has little medicinal use. In cookery, its flowers and young leaves can be added to salads and its crystallized blossoms used to decorate desserts and cakes. Its pretty, pale yellow flowers, which appear as a welcome sign of spring, mean that it has long been a popular ornamental plant.

PULMONARIA OFFICINALIS LUNGWORT

Native to Europe, lungwort grows in shady, moist grassland, hedgerows, and woods. Both the generic name "*Pulmonaria*" (derived from the Latin *pulmones*, meaning "lungs") and its common name lungwort refer to the mottled leaves' supposed resemblance to lungs. According to the *Doctrine of Signatures*, popular in sixteenth and seventeenth-century Europe, this meant the plant should be prescribed for lung complaints. It was traditionally used for these and to treat coughs, bronchitis, and sore throats. Today, it is little used medicinally but is an ingredient of the alcoholic drink vermouth.

OTHER NAMES: Jerusalem cowslip, soldiers and sailors

PLANT FAMILY: Boraginaceae

HEIGHT: 12in

HABIT: Hardy perennial with white-blotched, ovate, hairy, green leaves and bell-shaped flowers, changing from pink to blue

HABITAT: Moist soil in sun or shade

USES: Medicinal, culinary

PASQUE FLOWER PULSATILLA VULGARIS (ANEMONE PULSATILLA)

PLANT FAMILY:
  Ranunculaceae
HEIGHT: 4—8in, reaching
  16in when fruiting
HABIT: Hardy perennial
  with finely divided,
  green leaves and
  nodding, violet-colored
  flowers
HABITAT: Well-drained,
  neutral to alkaline soil
  in sun
USES: Medicinal, colorant

Native to Europe and Western Asia, pasque flower grows
on dry, chalky slopes but is now rare in the wild due to
over-harvesting. The plant's common name is linked to
paschal, meaning "of Easter," possibly due to the fact that
it flowers at Easter-time or because it yields a green dye,
a traditional color in Easter eggs. Medicinally, it was
used to relax spasms, relieve pain and pre-menstrual
tension, treat insomnia, and calm nervous tension.
Excessive use of the plant, however, can lead to
diarrhea, vomiting and, convulsions.

RICINUS COMMUNIS CASTOR OIL PLANT

Native to India, the castor oil plant is now naturalized in many parts of the tropics. The generic name *Ricinus* comes from the Latin for "tick," which the plant's seeds resemble. The plant has an ancient history, having been cultivated for over 6000 years. It was grown primarily for the oil from its seeds which was used as a lamp-oil in Ancient Egypt. Medicinally, it was always treated with huge caution as all parts of the plant, especially the ricin-rich seeds, are extremely toxic if eaten. Despite this, however, the plant was a traditional medicinal purgative. Today it is widely cultivated for its oil, used in the making of products as diverse as lubricating oils, varnishes, cosmetic, and dyes.

OTHER NAME: Palma-Christi
PLANT FAMILY:
  Euphorbiaceae
HEIGHT: 6ft
HABIT: Half-hardy shrub with large, palmate, lobed, toothed leaves and clusters of reddish flowers
HABITAT: Well-drained, humus-rich soil in sun
USES: Medicinal, cosmetic, industrial

DOG ROSE

ROSA CANINA

Native to Europe, West Asia, and North Africa, the dog rose grows wild in hedgerows and woods. Its curious common name may be a corruption of the Old French *dague*, meaning "dagger," a reference to its sharp thorns. Dog rosehips, high in vitamin C, have been eaten for thousands of years. Also high in calcium, phosphorus, and iron, they were traditionally taken to increase the body's resistance and to combat colds and flu. In country kitchens rosehips were traditionally used to make wine, vinegar, jams, jellies, syrup, and tea, all valued for their tonic effect. Rosehip syrup is today taken as a nutritional supplement, especially for children.

PLANT FAMILY: Rosaceae
HEIGHT: 10ft
HABIT: Hardy, deciduous shrub with prickly stems, pinnate leaves, divided into five to seven ovate green leaflets, and pale pink or white, five-petalled flowers
HABITAT: Well-drained, moist, humus-rich, neutral to slightly acid soil in sun
USES: Medicinal, culinary

ROSEMARY

ROSMARINUS OFFICINALIS

Native to the Mediterranean region, this aromatic plant grows wild on dry scrub and is also extensively cultivated. A great cosmetic and culinary herb, rosemary has many legendary associations. Perhaps the best-known story connected with it is a Christian one which tells how the Virgin Mary, during the flight to Egypt, flung her blue robe over a rosemary bush while resting; when she removed her cloak, the previously white flowers had turned blue in her honor. Another Christian legend has Mary spreading the infant Christ's clothes to dry on a rosemary bush, hence giving the plant its fragrance. Carrying a sprig of rosemary has long been seen as providing protection against evil. Rosemary, too, is a symbol of friendship, love, and fidelity. Thought to improve the memory, rosemary was also worn for remembrance, an association referred to by Shakespeare's Ophelia. Its aromatic leaves were used for strewing, burnt to purify the air, and in toilet waters and hair tonics. In the kitchen, rosemary is often cooked with lamb, its pungent fragrance cutting through the meat's rich fattiness. Because of the leaves' spikiness it is often used in sprig form, rather than chopped.

PLANT FAMILY: Lamiaceae
HEIGHT: Up to 6½ft
HABIT: Evergreen, hardy perennial with dark green, needle-shaped leaves and spires of small, blue-purple flowers
HABITAT: Well-drained to dry soil in the sun
USES: Culinary, cosmetic, decorative

BLACKBERRY RUBUS FRUCTICOSUS

OTHER NAME: Bramble
PLANT FAMILY: Rosaceae
HEIGHT: 12ft
HABIT: Hardy, semi-
evergreen shrub with
prickly stems, palmate
leaves with three to five
oval, toothed leaflets
and white or pink
flowers
HABITAT: Moist, well-
drained soil in sun
or shade
USES: Culinary, medicinal

Native to Europe, the blackberry grows wild in woods
and hedgerows and on waste ground. While its soft,
sweet berries have been valued as a foodstuff from man's
early history, it has also been prized medicinally. In
Ancient Greece it was used to treat gout, and in Ancient
Rome for bowel and mouth inflammations. It is a
traditional remedy for diarrhea and dysentery,
hemorrhoids, and cystitis. Known today primarily as a
culinary plant, blackberries can be eaten raw or cooked
in jams, jellies, syrups, and cordials. Blackberry leaves
are also used in herb teas.

RUMEX ACETOSA SORREL

Native to Europe, Asia and North America, sorrel grows widely in grassland and open woods. The common name "sorrel" is said to come from the Old French *surelle*, meaning "sour," a reference to the plant's tart flavor. It has been used since ancient times as both a culinary and a medicinal herb, eaten by the Ancient Eyptians and the Romans to aid digestion and used for blood-cleansing and diuretic and cooling purposes. Applied externally, it was a treatment for skin disorders such as sores, ringworm, and scabs. High in oxalic acid, sorrel should not consumed in excess; however, it is eaten in salads or cooked as a green vegetable, in omelettes or sauces.

OTHER NAMES: Common sorrel, garden sorrel, meadow sorrel, sour leaves, sour dock

PLANT FAMILY: Polygonaceae

HEIGHT: 20—48in

HABIT: Hardy perennial with broad, oblong, green leaves, arrow-shaped at the base and spikes of reddish-green flowers

HABITAT: Moist soil in sun or partial shade

USES: Culinary, medicinal

RUE

RUTA GRAVEOLENS

Native to Southern Europe, rue grows on dry, rocky slopes and limestone scree and has long been cultivated. Its generic name is from the Greek *reuo*, meaning "to set free," thought to refer to the plant's power to release people from disease. Its common name "herb of grace" derives from the tradition of using rue to sprinkle on holy water. Despite having toxic properties if taken in large quantities, there is a long history of this aromatic herb being used medicinally. It was a traditional treatment for strained eyes and for stimulating menstruation. Long thought of as a magical herb, offering protection against witchcraft, it was one of the herbs used in Four Thieves' Vinegar, drunk for protection against infection by thieves who plundered the bodies of plague victims. With its aromatic, bitter taste it is a flavoring for alcoholic drinks such as grappa.

OTHER NAMES: Herb of grace, herbygrass
PLANT FAMILY: Rutaceae
HEIGHT: 24in
HABIT: Hardy, evergreen perennial with deeply divided, fleshy, gray-green leaves and yellow, four-petalled flowers
HABITAT: Well-drained, neutral to alkaline soil in sun
USES: Medicinal, culinary

SAGE

SALVIA OFFICINALIS

Native to the Mediterranean and North Africa, sage is the commonly cultivated, best-known member of a large genus. It is a herb that has long been valued for its healing properties, as its Latin name *Salvia*, from the verb *salvere,* meaning "to save" indicates. An ancient proverb says simply, "Why should a man die who has sage in his garden?" The Romans and Greeks considered it efficacious against snake bites and for use in general tonics, while in medieval times it was a treatment for colds, fevers, epilepsy, and constipation. For centuries, country folk used sage in a variety of ways: for sage wine, sage tea, to flavor cheese, and in sage tobacco. It was also a mouthwash, a hair tonic, and rubbed on teeth to whiten them. Today, sage is thought of primarily as a culinary herb. In British cooking it adds its powerful, pungent flavor to traditional dishes such as sage and onion stuffing and Cumberland sausages. The Italians use sage widely, often combining it with meat as in *fegato alla salvia* (liver with sage) and in saltimbocca, where it flavors thinly sliced veal.

OTHER NAMES: Common sage, garden sage
PLANT FAMILY: Lamiaceae
HEIGHT: Up to 2ft
HABIT: Hardy perennial with oval, gray-green leaves and small spikes of purple-blue flowers
HABITAT: Full sun and well-drained to dry soil
USES: Culinary, medicinal

CLARY SAGE

SALVIA SCLAREA

Native to Southern Europe and West to Central Asia, clary sage grows wild in waste ground. Both its specific name *sclarea* and its common name derive from the Latin *clarus*, meaning "to clear," a reference to its properties as an eyewash. Its notable aromatic taste and scent meant that it was used to flavor Rhine wine in Germany, giving it a muscatel bouquet, hence the name "muscatel sage," Medicinally, it was prescribed to soothe eyes, aid digestion, and treat menstrual complaints. One traditional culinary use was to dip the leaves in batter and fry them as fritters. Its oil is used in the perfumery industry.

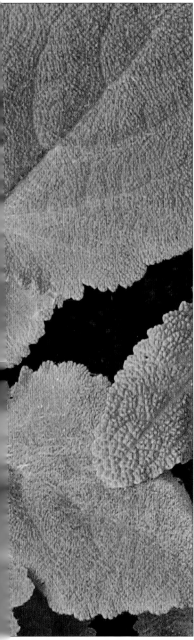

OTHER NAMES: Cleareye, muscatel sage
PLANT FAMILY: Lamiaceae
HEIGHT: 3ft
HABIT: hardy perennial or biennial with toothed, ovate to heart-shaped, green leaves and spikes of cream and lilac to pink or blue flowers
HABITAT: well-drained to dry, neutral to alkaline soil
USES: Culinary, medicinal, cosmetic

ELDER SAMBUCUS NIGRA

OTHER NAMES: Black elder, elderberry, European elder, bore tree

PLANT FAMILY: Caprifoliaceae

HEIGHT: 20—30ft

HABIT: Deciduous, hardy perennial with pinnate leaves, divided into five, ovate, green leaflets and flat-topped clusters of tiny, cream-colored flowers

HABITAT: Rich, moist, neutral to alkaline soil in sun or partial shade

USES: Culinary, medicinal

Native to Europe, West Asia, and North Africa, the elderflower grows wild in woods and hedgerows and on waste ground. Its generic name *Sambucus* apparently derives from the Greek *sambuca*, meaning "a musical pipe." Called "the medicine chest of the people" the elder has long been valued for its medicinal properties, taken internally for catarrh, colds and rheumatic complaints, and externally to soothe swellings, wounds, and bruises. There is much folklore associated with the plant in many cultures, including the Romany and Jewish. While the leaves and berries contain harmful toxins if eaten raw, the berries are traditionally used to make wine, chutneys, jellies, and ketchup. The fragrant flowers, too, can be made into cordial and "champagne," fritters, and they add a muscatel flavor to fruit-based desserts and jams.

SANGUISORBA MINOR SALAD BURNET

Found from Europe to China and Japan, salad burnet grows wild in grassy meadows and by roadsides. Its generic name comes from the Latin *sanguis sorbere*, meaning "to absorb blood" and refers to its traditional use as a wound herb, stanching bleeding. Medicinally, it was also used as a mild diuretic, in tea form, to promote perspiration and to aid digestion. As its common name implies there is a long tradition of eating its cucumber-flavored leaves in salads, especially in the winter when green leaves were scarce. It was also infused in wine cups, beer, and cold drinks and added to soups and stews.

OTHER NAMES: Old man's pepper, poor man's pepper, small burnet
PLANT FAMILY: Rosaceae
HEIGHT: 16—30in
HABIT: Evergreen, hardy perennial with pinnate leaves divided into three to seven pairs of oval, deeply toothed, green leaflets and spikes of tiny, maroon flowers
HABITAT: Moist, well-drained soil in sun or partial shade
USES: Culinary, medicinal

COTTON LAVENDER

SANTOLINA CHAMAECYPARISSUS

Native to the Mediterranean, cotton lavender grows wild on chalky waste ground. The generic name comes from the Latin *sanctum linum*, meaning "holy flax." A bitter herb, with a strong camomile-like scent, it was used medicinally to expel intestinal worms, treat digestive problems, and soothe sore eyes. The seventeenth-century herbalist Nicholas Culpeper recommended it as a remedy for poisonous bites and skin irritations. Dried sprigs were kept in linen chests and added to herb sachets to deter moths and other insects. Its silvery-gray foliage made it a popular plant for hedging knot gardens during the sixteenth century. Today it is valued primarily as an ornamental plant.

OTHER NAME: Santolina
PLANT FAMILY: Asteraceae
HEIGHT: 8—20in
HABIT: Hardy evergreen perennial with silver-gray, woolly, linear, lobed leaves and yellow button flowers
HABITAT: Light, well-drained to dry soil in sun
USES: Medicinal, decorative

SOAPWORT SAPONARIA OFFICINALIS

OTHER NAME: Bouncing bet
PLANT FAMILY: Caryophyllaceae
HEIGHT: 12—36in
HABIT: Hardy perennial with opposite, ovate, pointed, green leaves and clusters of pink or white flowers
HABITAT: Well-drained, moist, neutral to alkaline soil in sun or partial shade
USES: Medicinal, cleaning

Native to Europe, soapwort is found growing on roadside verges or in waste ground. Both its generic name *Saponaria* (derived from the Latin *sapo*, meaning "soap") and its common name "soapwort" refer to the plant's traditional use for cleaning. High in saponin, with lathering properties, it has been used for washing for centuries, with the Assyrians in the eighth century BC using it as a soap. It is particularly suited to washing delicate fabrics and for cleaning pictures, tapestries, and furniture and is made use of by museums today. In England it was often grown near woolen mills to clean cloth before the advent of commercially produced soap. Medicinally, it was valued as a treatment for gout, rheumatism, jaundice, and venereal disease but is not often used today because of its irritant effects on the digestive system and the risk of muscular paralysis.

SATUREJA HORTENSIS SUMMER SAVORY

Native to the Mediterranean, summer savory grows wild on mountainsides and moorland, but is cultivated primarily as a potherb. The generic name *Satureja* comes from the Latin *satyrus*, meaning "satyr," a reference to the plant's supposed aphrodisiac properties. Medicinally, summer savory was used to regulate the digestive system, as an expectorant and a wash for mouth ulcers. Primarily, however, it has always been seen as a culinary herb, with the Romans adding it as an aromatic, peppery flavor to sauces and stuffings. It is traditionally cooked with foods which are hard to digest, such as beans (hence the name "bean herb"), pork, and cucumber. In French cuisine it is one of the herbs used in *herbes de Provence*.

OTHER NAME: Bean herb
PLANT FAMILY: Lamiaceae
HEIGHT: 4—14in
HABIT: Hardy annual with linear to oblong, pointed, green leaves and small white, pink or lilac flowers
HABITAT: Well-drained to dry, neutral to alkaline soil in sun
USES: Culinary, medicinal

WINTER SAVORY SATUREJA MONTANA

OTHER NAME: Mountain savory

PLANT FAMILY: Lamiaceae

HEIGHT: 4—16in

HABIT: Semi-evergreen, hardy, perennial sub-shrub with leathery, linear, dark green leaves and small, white to purple flowers

HABITAT: Well-drained to dry, neutral to alkaline soil in sun

USES: Culinary, decorative

Native to Southern Europe, winter savory grows wild on rocky mountain slopes and dry, sunny places. Similar in flavor to thyme, European savories have been used as herbs for over 2000 years, Known by the Ancient Romans and the Greeks, they were primarily seen as culinary herbs rather than medicinal ones, with winter savory and summer savory (*Satureja hortensis*) being the best-known species. Winter savory has a sharper, spicier, more pungent taste than summer savory and is added to stuffings, marinades, and pickles. Its shrubby qualities mean that winter savory can be planted as a dwarf hedge or edging plant.

SCUTELLARIA LATERIFLORA VIRGINIA SKULLCAP

Native to North America, the Virginia skullcap grows wild in damp places. Its medicinal properties were long known to the Native American tribes, with the Cherokees using it to treat menstrual problems. It is a bitter herb that acts as a sedative, relaxes spasms, lowers fevers, and stimulates the kidneys. Its fame spread during the eighteenth-century when Dr Vandesveer used it as a treatment for rabies, hence its common name "mad dog skullcap." During the nineteenth-century it was a treatment for hysterical and nervous complaints, such as convulsions, hysterics, and epilepsy.

OTHER NAME: Mad dog skullcap
PLANT FAMILY: Lamiaceae
HEIGHT: 6—30in
HABIT: Hardy perennial with ovate-lanceolate, toothed, green leaves and small blue or pink or white flowers
HABITAT: Damp soil in sun or partial shade
USES: Medicinal

MILK THISTLE

SILYBUM MARIANUM

Native to Europe, the milk thistle grows wild along roadsides or on waste ground. Its specific name *marianum* derives from the legend that the Virgin Mary's milk ran down its leaves, causing their striking white stains. As its name suggests, it was traditionally thought to be good for breast-feeding women, encouraging their milk. Medicinally, the plant was used to treat depression, with the sixteenth-century herbalist John Gerard calling it "the best remedy that grows against all melancholy diseases." Research has shown it to be high in a flavonolignan called silymarin which protects the liver against toxins, making it an effective treatment for animals or people poisoned by the death cap mushroom. Its young leaves, trimmed of their spines, can be eaten as a salad or a cooked vegetable and its roots, too, can be cooked and eaten.

OTHER NAMES: Blessed thistle, Our Lady's thistle
PLANT FAMILY: Asteraceae
HEIGHT: 4—5ft
HABIT: Hardy annual or biennial with white-veined, deeply lobed, crinkly leaves with spiny margins and purple, thistle-like flowers
HABITAT: Well-drained, neutral to alkaline soil in sun
USES: Culinary, medicinal

GOLDENROD

SOLIDAGO VIRGAUREA

Native to Europe, goldenrod grows in the wild in waste ground and on hillsides, especially where the ground is rich in silica. The generic name *Solidago* derives from the Latin *solidare*, meaning "to join," a reference to the plant's healing powers. During the Middle Ages when it was brought back from the Crusades to England it was known as "heathen wound herb." Its leaves and flowers are used particularly to treat kidney stones and also, according to the seventeenth-century herbalist Culpeper, to fasten loose teeth. A bitter, astringent, relaxant herb it stimulates the liver and kidneys and reduces inflammation. Externally, it was used in compresses to treat wounds and insect bites.

OTHER NAME: European goldenrod
PLANT FAMILY: Asteraceae
HEIGHT: 32in
HABIT: Hardy perennial with lance-shaped, finely toothed, green leaves and yellow flowers
HABITAT: Well-drained, sandy to poor soil in sun
USES: Medicinal

BETONY STACHYS OFFICINALIS

OTHER NAMES:
Bishopswort, wood betony
PLANT FAMILY: Lamiaceae
HEIGHT: 6—24in
HABIT: Hardy perennial with oblong, scallop-edged, green leaves and spikes of magenta flowers
HABITAT: Well-drained soil in sun or partial shade
USES: Medicinal

Native to Europe, betony grows wild in fields and hedgerows and is popular in wildflower meadows. The generic name *Stachys* derives from the Greek word for an ear of corn, referring to the plant's flowering spikes. The Ancient Egyptians attributed magical properties to this herb and for centuries it was regarded as possessing special properties, with the Anglo-Saxons using it against Elf sickness. It was cultivated in physic gardens, monastery gardens, and also grown in church grounds and graveyards to offer protection against witchcraft. In traditional medicine it was used to treat a wide range of ailments and sicknesses, including head colds, sore throats, gout, and nervous conditions. Today it has little used medicinal application, but its dried leaves are an ingredient in herbal tobacco and snuff.

STELLARIA MEDIA CHICKWEED

Native to Europe, this widespread weed grows in fields, yards and on waste ground. The Latin name *Stellaria* is a reference to its little, white, star-shaped flowers. As its common name "chickweed" indicates it is indeed happily eaten by chickens, and for many centuries by humans too. During the Middle Ages it was added raw to salads or cooked as a vegetable, similar to spinach, or used in soups. Today it is also liquidized with other herbs and vegetables as a tonic. It was valued for its soothing and cooling properties, traditionally used in poultices or ointments to treat irritated skin, chilblains, and ulcers. The seventeenth-century herbalist Culpeper recommended its juice to treat sore eyes. Today, however, it is generally regarded as a troublesome weed.

OTHER NAMES: Starweed, winterweed
PLANT FAMILY: Caryophyllaceae
HEIGHT: 2—16in
HABIT: Half-hardy annual with small, light green, ovate leaves and small, starry white flowers
HABITAT: Moist soil in sun or shade
USES: Medicinal, culinary

COMFREY SYMPHYTUM OFFICINALE

OTHER NAMES: Boneset, bruisewort, knitbone
PLANT FAMILY: Boraginaceae
HEIGHT: Up to 4ft
HABIT: Hardy perennial with large, pointed, ovate-lanceolate leaves and white, pink or purple bell-like flowers
HABITAT: Moist to wet soil in sun or partial shade
USES: Medicinal

Native to Europe and West Asia, comfrey grows wild in damp, shady places, particularly near streams and rivers. Both the Roman name *conferva*, meaning "join together" (from which comfrey derives) and the generic name , from the Greek *sympho* meaning "to unite," refer to the plant's healing properties, as do its other common names. For centuries it was used to treat wounds and help broken bones set. The seventeenth-century herbalist Culpeper wrote of it being "special good for ruptures and broken bones." Research has discovered that comfrey contains allantoin, which actively promotes the growth of new cells. It has also, however, been connected to liver damage and cancer so its internal consumption is subject to restrictions. Externally, however, it is still used in herbal medicine, particularly for bruises, sprains, and wounds.

TANACETUM BALSAMITA COSTMARY

Thought to have originated in Asia, costmary was introduced into Europe and North America, where it now grows wild. The common name "costmary" derives from the Sanskrit *kustha*, meaning "aromatic plant" and the Virgin Mary to whom the plant was dedicated. Its aromatic leaves, with their balsam fragrance, made it a popular herb for flavoring and preserving beer, hence another of its common names, "alecost." Its pressed leaves were made into fragrant bookmarks, which is why it was also called "bibleleaf." In traditional medicine it was used in herb teas to ease the pain of childbirth and as a liver remedy. Today, it remains a popular ingredient in potpourri.

OTHER NAMES: Alecost, balsam herb, bibleleaf
PLANT FAMILY: Asteraceae
HEIGHT: 36in
HABIT: Hardy perennial with oblong, silvery-green leaves and clusters of daisy-like flowers
HABITAT: Well-drained to dry, stony soil in sun
USES: Medicinal, culinary, decorative

FEVERFEW

TANACETUM PARTHENIUM

Native to Europe, feverfew can be found in hedgerows and waste ground and is cultivated as an ornamental plant. The plant's common name "feverfew" refers to its historic, medicinal use as a treatment for fevers. The seventeenth-century herbalist Culpeper noted it as being particularly good for female conditions and also as "very effectual for all pains in the head." Clinical studies have shown that the herb can indeed help migraine sufferers, with two or three leaves of the fresh herb consumed directly, although its bitter taste is not particularly palatable.

OTHER NAME: Featherfew
PLANT FAMILY: Asteraceae
HEIGHT: Up to 3ft
HABIT: Hardy perennial with deeply-cut, yellow-green leaves and clusters of daisy-like flowers
HABITAT: Well-drained to dry, stony soil in sun
USES: Medicinal, decorative

TANSY

TANACETUM VULGARE
(CHRYSANTHEMUM VULGARE)

Native to Europe, tansy grows in the wild on waste ground and in hedgerows and is cultivated as an ornamental plant. The name "tansy" derives from the Greek *athanasia*, meaning "immortality," possibly because of the custom of packing dead bodies with tansy leaves to help preserve them until burial. With its pungent-smelling leaves, tansy was long used as a strewing herb and an insecticide. Medicinally, it was valued as a tonic and stimulant, used as an enema to expel worms and for menstrual problems, though it is now considered dangerous as tansy oil is highly toxic. It is also a herb with a long history of culinary use, with its peppery leaves added to flavor custards, cakes, and puddings in medieval times.

OTHER NAME: Bachelor's buttons
PLANT FAMILY: Asteraceae
HEIGHT: 2—4ft
HABIT: Hardy perennial with finely divided, feathery green leaves and clusters of yellow, button-like flowers
HABITAT: Well-drained to dry, stony soil in sun
USES: Culinary, medicinal, insecticide

A Pocket Guide to Herbs

DANDELION TARAXACUM OFFICINALE

OTHER NAMES: Fairy clock, piss-a-beds, blowballs
PLANT FAMILY: Asteraceae
HEIGHT: 12in
HABIT: Hardy perennial with lance-shaped, toothed, green leaves and yellow flowers
HABITAT: Any soil in sun or partial shade
USES: Culinary, medicinal

Native throughout the Northern Hemisphere, the dandelion grows commonly in the wild, found by roadsides, in meadows, and on waste land and lawns. The common name comes from its former Latin name, *dens leonis*, meaning "lion's tooth," a reference to the plant's jagged leaf. Despite being commonly dismissed as a weed, it has a long history of medicinal and culinary use, promoted by Arab physicians in the eleventh century. It is a powerful diuretic, hence the common name "piss-a-beds." In Chinese medicine it is used to treat tumors, abscesses, jaundice, and urinary tract infections. It has also long been valued as a nutritious salad vegetable, rich in vitamins and minerals, often eaten blanched to lessen its bitterness. Its roasted, ground roots are a traditional, caffeine-free substitute for coffee.

TEUCRIUM CHAMAEDRYS WALL GERMANDER

Native to Europe and South-West Asia, wall germander grows wild in dry, sunny waste ground or on sheltered walls and steep banks. Its history of medicinal use goes back to the days of the Ancient Greeks, with Dioscorides recommending it as a treatment for coughs and asthma. During the sixteenth century, the Holy Roman Emperor Charles V was said to have been cured of gout after taking it for sixty days. The seventeenth-century herbalist Culpeper recommended a decoction of its leaves for treating several ills, including those of the brain such as headaches and epilepsy. It is now linked to liver damage and its internal use is restricted in some countries.

PLANT FAMILY: Lamiaceae
HEIGHT: 4—10in
HABIT: Hardy perennial with ovate, deeply veined, green leaves and spikes of small, two-lipped, pink flowers
HABITAT: Light, well-drained, neutral to alkaline, stony soil in sun
USES: Medicinal

WOOD SAGE

TEUCRIUM SCORODONIA

Native to Europe, wood sage grows in the wild in a variety of habitats including woodland, heathland, and dunes. The generic name *Teucrium* is thought to refer either to a mythological archer at Troy named Teucer or a medical botanist called Dr. Teucer. In traditional herbal medicine it was particularly valued as a tonic, helping to restore the appetite, especially after attacks of rheumatism or gout. It was also used as a diuretic and to restore menstrual flow and dispel clotted blood beneath bruises. Its bitter leaves, with their hop-like smell and flavor, were a traditional additive in brewing ale and it can be eaten in salads when young and tender.

OTHER NAMES: Mountain sage, sage-leaved germander
PLANT FAMILY: Lamiaceae
HEIGHT: 12—24in
HABIT: Hardy perennial with coarsely toothed, heart-shaped, grayish-green leaves and small, yellowish-green flowers
HABITAT: Light, well-drained, neutral to alkaline, dry or stony soil in sun
USES: Culinary, medicinal

THYME

THYMUS VULGARIS

Native to the Mediterranean, common thyme grows in the wild on rocky ground and is widely cultivated. Its aromatic leaves and antiseptic properties meant that it was used by the Ancient Egyptians in oil form for embalming and by the Ancient Greeks and Romans to perfume baths and to purify rooms. During the Middle Ages, it was carried in posies to ward off disease and modern research has shown thyme oil to be very effective against bacilli. Medicinally, it was a treatment for coughs and digestive disorders. It is a well-known and widely used culinary herb. In French cuisine it is a key ingredient of *bouquets garni* and *herbes de Provence* and it adds flavor to stews, braised dishes, soups as well as fish, meat, and vegetable dishes.

OTHER NAME: Garden thyme
PLANT FAMILY: Lamiaceae
HEIGHT: 6—12in
HABIT: Hardy perennial with small, linear to elliptic, pointed, gray-green leaves and small purple to white flowers
HABITAT: Light, dry, well-drained soil in sun or partial shade
USES: Culinary, medicinal, cosmetic

LIME TILIA CORDATA

OTHER NAMES: Linden, leaf linden
PLANT FAMILY: Tiliaceae
HEIGHT: 70—130ft
HABIT: Hardy tree with dark green, shiny, heart-shaped leaves and clusters of small, pale yellow blossoms
HABITAT: Moist, well-drained soil in sun or partial shade
USES: Medicinal, decoratives

Native to Europe, the lime tree has been widely planted in European towns and cities in parks, gardens, and along avenues and streets. The Romans planted lime trees in their towns, believing that the tree induced calm. Medicinally, the lime tree has been used for centuries, with the Roman naturalist Pliny recommending vinegar infused with lime tree bark as a treatment for blemishes. Centuries later, the herbalist Culpeper wrote of lime being "excellent for apoplexy, epilepsy, vertigo, and palpitation of the heart." The tree is best-known for the tisane made from its fragrant flowers, fresh or dried, drunk particularly at night after a meal to aid digestion and to calm the nerves.

TRIGONELLA FOENUM-GRAECUM FENUGREEK

Native to Southern Europe and Asia, fenugreek is widely cultivated as a fodder crop and for culinary and medicinal reasons. The specific name *foenum-graecum* means "Greek hay," from its use in ancient times as cattle fodder. It has a venerable history of medicinal use, mentioned as a herb to induce childbirth in a papyrus dating back to c.1500 BC and used today in Egypt to treat painful menstruation. Long known in both Ayurvedic and Chinese medicine, fenugreek is given to treat kidney-related disorders, loss of libido, and digestive and bronchial complaints. It is a widely used culinary herb, with both its leaves and its seeds used in a number countries. It features particularly in Indian cuisine, where fresh fenugreek (known as "methi"), with its distinctive bitter taste, is a popular vegetable while its dried seeds are added as a spice to flavor curries, chutneys, and pickles.

PLANT FAMILY:
Papilonaceae

HEIGHT: 24in

HABIT: Hardy annual with trifoliate leaves divided into oval, green, toothed leaflets and yellow-white flowers

HABITAT: Well-drained, fertile soil in sun

USES: Culinary, medicinal

NASTURTIUM

TROPAEOLUM MAJUS

Native to South America, the nasturtium was introduced to Europe by the Spanish conquistadors in the sixteenth century and is now widely cultivated in many countries around the world. The generic name *Tropaeolum* comes from the Greek *tropaion*, meaning "trophy," a reference to the shield-shaped leaves and helmet-like flowers. Medicinally, nasturtiums were used to treat urinary infections and influenza. The plant was also considered to have tonic properties and, in hair lotion form, to help prevent baldness. The peppery leaves, flowers, and flower buds are eaten in salads or sandwiches, while the flowers are added to flavor vinegar and the unripe seeds pickled as a substitute for capers. With its bright, decorative flowers, the nasturtium is today a popular ornamental plant.

OTHER NAME: Indian cress
PLANT FAMILY: Tropaeolaceae
HEIGHT: 10ft
HABIT: Half-hardy to tender annual with rounded leaves and large orange, red, or yellow flowers
HABITAT: Well-drained, moist, poor to average soil in sun
USES: Culinary, medicinal, decorative, cosmetic

COLTSFOOT TUSSILAGO FARFARA

PLANT FAMILY: Asteraceae
HEIGHT: 12in
HABIT: Hardy perennial with large, toothed, heart-shaped, green leaves and solitary, yellow flowers
HABITAT: Moist, neutral to alkaline soil in sun or partial shade
USES: Medicinal, culinary

Native to Europe, West Asia, and North Africa, the coltsfoot grows in the wild in hedgerows and on fields, banks, and waste ground. The generic name *Tussilago* is said to derive from the Latin *tussis*, meaning "to cough," a reference to the plant's long use as a treatment for coughs. Medicinally, its leaves, flowers, and mucilaginous roots were all traditionally used as a soothing expectorant, taken in the form of a herb tea, decoction, or syrup. The Roman naturalist Pliny recommended that the herb be burned and its smoke swallowed to relieve coughs. Coltsfoot is also a treatment in Chinese medicine for coughs. Its culinary uses included adding its young leaves and buds to salads and soups and for tea, while its flowers were used to make country wine.

URTICA DIOICA STINGING NETTLE

Native to Eurasia, the stinging nettle grows commonly in the wild, found in hedgerows, grassy places, and waste ground. The generic name *Urtica* comes from the Latin *urere*, meaning "to burn," a reference to the plant's notorious stinging properties. Today, the nettle is often dismissed simply as an unwanted weed, yet, in fact, it has an ancient history as a useful herb. Medicinally, the stinging nettle was valued for its astringent, tonic, anti-asthmatic, and diuretic properties, in the treatment of rheumatism, kidney stones, nosebleeds, and mouth ulcers. Nettle-leaf tea was a traditional tonic treatment for dull hair and dandruff. High in vitamins A and C and minerals, particularly iron, it was long used as a nutritious culinary plant, particularly in soups or cooked as a green vegetable. Nettle fiber was also important in cloth manufacture for several centuries until the early twentieth century.

OTHER NAMES: Common nettle, nettle
PLANT FAMILY: Urticaceae
HEIGHT: 5ft
HABIT: Hardy perennial with ovate, pointed, deeply toothed green leaves and tiny green flowers
HABITAT: Moist, nitrogen-rich soil in sun or dappled shade
USES: Medicinal, culinary, cosmetic, clothing

VALERIAN

VALERIANA OFFICINALIS

Native to Europe, valerian grows wild by
streams and ditches, and on roadside verges.
The generic name may come from the Latin
valere, meaning "to be in health," a reference
to its healing properties. It has a long
history of medicinal use, notably
recommended by Hippocrates in the fourth
century BC. During the Middle Ages it was
known as "all-heal" and regarded as a
panacea, widely grown in monastery
gardens. With its calming and sedative
properties valerian root was employed over
the centuries to treat conditions including
epilepsy, insomnia, hysteria, and migraines.
Native Americans used a local species of
valerian to heal cuts and wounds. During
World War I, tincture of valerian was
prescribed for shell shock. Dried valerian
root, with a distinctive smell that appeals to
cats, was traditionally used in linen chests.

OTHER NAMES: All-heal, common valerian, garden
heliotrope
PLANT FAMILY: Valerianaceae
HEIGHT: 5ft
HABIT: Hardy perennial with pinnate leaves divided into
seven to ten pairs of leaflets (often toothed) and
clusters of tiny pink, lilac, or white flowers
HABITAT: Moist soil in sun or shade
USES: Medicinal

GREAT MULLEIN VERBASCUM THAPSUS

OTHER NAMES: Aaron's rod, candlewick plant
PLANT FAMILY: Scrophulariaceae
HEIGHT: 6ft
HABIT: Hardy biennial with long, oblong-ovate, gray-green, woolly leaves and spikes of five-petalled, yellow flowers
HABITAT: Well-drained to poor dry soil in sun
USES: Medicinal

Native to Europe and naturalized in North America, great mullein grows wild on sunny banks, waste ground, and roadside verges. Its common name "Aaron's rod" refers to its tall, upright, striking appearance while "candlewick" refers to the traditional use of its stalks as candles. This bitter-tasting, mucilaginous herb, with its soothing and antiseptic properties, has long been used medicinally, particularly for treating chest complaints ranging from sore throats and hoarseness to tonsillitis and asthma. In ointment or compress form it is applied externally to treat earache, sores, hemorrhoids, boils, chilblains, and rheumatic pains. Its dried leaves are added to herbal cigarettes. Since ancient times, great mullein has been thought to have the power to drive away evil spirits.

VERBENA OFFICINALIS **VERVAIN**

Native to Europe, West Asia and North Africa, verbena grows in the wild along roadsides and on waste ground. It is a herb with many legendary and mythic associations, regarded as magical by the Ancient Druids and used as an altar plant by the Romans. Christian folklore tells of it growing on Calgary, used to stanch Christ's blood at the Crucifixion. Medicinally, it was seen as something of a cure-all, with the seventeenth-century herbalist Culpeper recommending it for ailments including jaundice, dropsy, gout, coughs, and diseases of the liver. It was also long thought to be an aphrodisiac. Today, vervain is grown mainly for medicinal purposes, used in western medicine it is prescribed for the treatment of nervous complaints and for liver, spleen, and bladder conditions in Chinese medicine.

OTHER NAMES: European vervain, simpler's joy, turkey grass
PLANT FAMILY: Verbenaceae
HEIGHT: 32in
HABIT: Hardy perennial with deeply lobed, green leaves and spikes of small, mauve flowers
HABITAT: Well-drained, moist soil in sun
USES: Medicinal

HEARTSEASE

VIOLA TRICOLOR

Found as a wildflower in Europe and North America, heartsease grows wild in grassland or on waste ground and is also cultivated. Its specific name *tricolor* refers to its distinctive, three-colored flowers, combining purple, white, and yellow. During the Middle Ages it was known as "trinitaria," the herb of the Blessed Trinity, because of its coloring. It is a herb with a long history of romantic connotations, used as a love charm, as a heart cordial, and to cure broken hearts. Medicinal applications for heartsease include treating eczema, soothing rheumatic pains and, in syrup form, as a cough medicine. It is a mild diuretic and can be used to cleanse the body and stimulate the metabolism. Its pretty flowers can be added to salads, used to garnish dishes, or frozen in ice cubes to decorate drinks.

OTHER NAMES: Love-lies-bleeding, wild pansy
PLANT FAMILY: Violaceae
HEIGHT: 6—12in
HABIT: Hardy annual, biennial or short-lived perennial with heart-shaped, toothed, green leaves and purple, white, and yellow-colored flowers
HABITAT: Well-drained, moist, humus-rich soil in sun or partial shade
USES: Culinary, medicinal, decorative

VIOLET

VIOLA ODORATA

Native to Europe, the violet grows wild in fields and hedgerows and is also widely cultivated. This pretty herb has long been valued for its scented flowers, perfuming wine, sweets, cosmetics, and medicines since classical times. In Greek legend, the violet is the flower of Aphrodite, the Goddess of Love, used in love potions and to promote fertility. The Ancient Greeks and Romans drank violet wine, thought to be good for hangovers. Medicinally, violets were a traditional remedy for hangovers, migraine, and insomnia. A soothing expectorant, violet tea or syrup was a treatment for sore throats, whooping cough, and chest complaints. In the past scented violets were cultivated on a large scale for their essential oil, used in perfumery and cosmetics, but today this essence is largely synthesised chemically.

OTHER NAME: Sweet violet
PLANT FAMILY: Violaceae
HEIGHT: 6in
HABIT: Hardy, semi-evergreen perennial with dark green, heart-shaped leaves and deep purple or white flowers
HABITAT: Well-drained, humus-rich, moist soil in sun or partial shade
USES: Medicinal, culinary, cosmetic, decorative

APPENDICES

Scientific Name	Common Name	Uses
Achillea ageratum	English Mace	Culinary, medicinal
Achillea millefolium	Yarrow	Culinary, medicinal, cosmetic
Aconitum napellus	Monkshood	Medicinal
Agastache foeniculum	Anise Hyssop	Culinary, decorative, medicinal
Agrimonia eupatoria	Agrimony	Medicinal
Ajuga reptans	Bugle	Medicinal, decorative
Alchemilla xanhochlora (Alchemilla vulgaris)	Lady's Mantle	Medicinal
Alliaria petiolata	Jack-by-the-Hedge	Culinary, medicinal
Allium sativum	Garlic	Culinary, medicinal
Allium schoenoprasum	Chives	Culinary, medicinal
Allium tuberosum	Chinese Chives	Culinary, medicinal
Allium ursinum	Ramsoss	Culinary, medicinal
Aloe vera (A.barbadensis)	Aloe Vera	Medicinal
Aloysia triphylla	Lemon Verbena	Culinary, medicinal, cosmetic
Althaea officinalis	Marsh Mallow	Culinary, medicinal, cosmetic
Anethum graveolens	Dill	Culinary, medicinal
Angelica archangelica	Angelica	Culinary, cosmetic
Anthriscus cerefolium	Chervil	Culinary, medicinal
Apium graveolens	Wild Celery	Culinary, medicinal
Arctium lappa	Burdock	Culinary, medicinal
Arisaema triphyllum	Jack-in-the-Pulpit	Medicinal culinary, decorative
Aristolochia	Birthwort	Medicinal
Armoracia rusticana (A. lapathifolia, Cochlearia armoracia)	Horseradish	Culinary, medicinal
Arnica montana	Arnica	Medicinal
Artemisia brotanum	Southernwood	Culinary, medicinal, decorative, repellent
Artemisia absinthium	Wormwood	Medicinal
Artemisia dranculus	Tarragon	Culinary, medicinal
Artemisia vulgaris	Mugwort	Culinary, medicinal

Scientific Name	Common Name	Uses
Atropa belladonna	Deadly Nightshade	Medicinal
Bellis perennis	Daisy	Culinary, medicinal
Borago officinalis	Borage	Culinary, medicinal
Buxus sempervirens	Box	Medicinal, wood
Calamintha grandiflora	Calamint	Medicinal, decorative
Calendula officinalis	Marigold	Culinary, medicinal, cosmetic, colorant
Cardamine pratensis	Lady's Smock	Culinary, medicinal
Carthamus tinctorius	Safflower	Culinary, colorant
Carum carvi	Caraway	Culinary, medicinal
Centaurium erythraea	Centaury	Medicinal
Chamaemelum nobile	Chamomile	Medicinal, culinary, decorative
Chenopodium bonus-henricus	Good King Henry	Culinary, medicinal, colorant
Cichorium intybus	Chicory	Culinary, medicinal
Citrus hystrix	kaffir Lime	Culinary, medicinal
Claytonia perfoliata	Winter Purslane	Medicinal
Convallaria majalis	Lily-of-the-Valley	Medicinal
Coriandrum sativum	Coriander	Culinary, medicinal
Cymbopogon citratus	Lemon Grass	Culinary, medicinal, repellent
Dianthus caryophyllus	Clove Pink	Culinary, medicinal, decorative
Dictamnus albus	White Dittany	Medicinal, decorative
Digitalis purpurea	Foxglove	Medicinal, decorative
Drosera rotundifolia	Sundew	Medicinal, decorative
Echium vulgare	Viper's Bugloss	Culinary, medicinal
Echinacea purpurea	Echinacea	Medicinal, decorative
Equisetum arvense	Horsetail	Medicinal
Eruca vesicaria	Salad Rocket	Culinary
Eryngium maritimum	Sea Holly	Medicinal, culinary, decorative
Eschscholzia californica	California Poppy	Medicinal, culinary

Scientific Name	Common Name	Uses
Eucalyptus globulus	Eucalyptus	Medicinal, decorative
Eupatorium purpurea	Jo Pye Weed	Medicinal, decorative
Filipendula ulmaria (Spirea ulmaria)	Meadowsweet	Culinary, medicinal
Foeniculum vulgare	Fennel	Culinary, medicinal, decorative
Fragaria vesca	Wild Strawberry	Culinary, medicinal
Fumaria officinalis	Fumitory	Medicinal
Galega officinalis	Goat's Rue	Medicinal
Galium odoratum	Sweet Woodruff	Medicinal, culinary, repellent
Galium verum	Lady's Bedstraw	Culinary, medicinal colorant
Gardenia augusta	Gardenia	Medicinal, decorative, colorant
Gaultheria procumbens	Wintergreen	Medicinal, culinary
Gentiana lutea	Yellow Gentian	Medicinal, culinary
Glycyrrhiza glabra	Liquorice	Culinary, medicinal
Hamamelis virginiana	Witch Hazel	Medicinal, decorative
Helichrysum Italicum (augustifolium)	Curry Plant	Culinary, decorative
Helleborus niger	Christmas Rose	Medicinal
Humulus lupulus	Hops	Culinary, medicinal, decorative
Hyoscyamus niger	Henbane	Medicinal
Hypericum perforatum	St John's Wort	Medicinal, decorative
Hyssopus officinalis	Hyssop	Culinary, medicinal, cosmetic
Inula helenium	Elecampane	Medicinal, decorative
Iris germanica var. florentina	Orris	Culinary, medicinal, cosmetic, decorative
Juniperus communis	Juniper	Medicinal, culinary

Scientific Name	Common Name	Uses
Lamium album	White Deadnettle	Culinary, medicinal
Laurus nobilis	Bay	Culinary, medicinal
Lavandula angustifolia	Lavender	Culinary, medicinal, cosmetic, repellent
Lepidium sativum	Cress	Culinary, medicinal
Levisticum officinale	Lovage	Culinary, medicinal
Linum usitatissimum	Flax	Culinary, medicinal
Lonicera periclymenum	Honeysuckle	Medicinal, cosmetic
Lythrum salicaria	Purple Loosestrife	Medicinal
Marrubium vulgare	White Horehound	Culinary, medicinal
Melissa officinalis	Lemon Balm	Culinary, medicinal
Mentha pulegium	Pennyroyal	Culinary, medicinal, repellent
Mentha spicata	Spearmint	Culinary, medicinal, repellent
Mentha x piperita	Peppermint	Culinary, medicinal
Monarda didyma	Bergamot	Culinary, medicinal
Murraya koenigii	Curry Leaf	Culinary, medicinal, decorative
Myrrhis odorata	Sweet Cicely	Culinary, medicinal, decorative
Myrtus communis	Myrtle	Culinary, medicinal, decorative
Nasturtium officinale (Rorippa nasturtium-aquaticum)	Watercress	Culinary, medicinal
Nepeta cataria	Catnip	Culinary, medicinal
Ocimum basilicum	Basil	Culinary, medicinal
Oenothera biennis	Evening Primrose	Medicinal
Origanum majorana	Sweet Marjoram	Culinary, medicinal
Origanum vulgare	Oregano	Culinary, medicinal, cosmetic
Papaver somniferum	Opium Poppy	Culinary, medicinal
Pelargonium capitatum	Rose-scented Geranium	Medicinal, cosmetic

Scientific Name	Common Name	Uses
Perilla frutescens (Perilla ocimodes)	Shiso	Culinary, medicinal
Petroselinum crispum	Parsley	Culinary, medicinal
Petroselinum crispum French	Flat-leafed Parsley	Culinary, medicinal
Polygonatum odoratum	Solomon's seal	Medicinal, decorative
Portulaca oleracea	Purslane	Culinary, medicinal
Potentilla erecta	Cinquefoil	Medicinal, colorant
Primula veris	Cowslip	Culinary, medicinal
Primula vulgaris	Primrose	Culinary, medicinal
Pulmonaria officinalis	Lungwort	Medicinal, culinary
Pulsatilla vulgaris (Anemone pulsatilla)	Pasque Flower	Medicinal, colourant
Ricinus communis	Castor Oil Plant	Culinary, medicinal, cosmetic, industrial
Rosa canina	Dog Rose	Medicinal, culinary
Rosmarinus officinalis	Rosemary	Culinary, cosmetic, decorative
Rubus fructicosus	Blackberry	Culinary, medicinal
Rumex acetosa	Sorrel	Culinary, medicinal
Ruta graveolens	Rue	Medicinal, culinary
Salvia officinalis	Sage	Culinary, medicinal
Salvia sclarea	Clary Sage	Culinary, medicinal, cosmetic
Sambucus nigra	Elder	Culinary, medicinal
Sanguisorba minor	Salad Burnet	Culinary, medicinal
Santolina chamaecyparissus	Cotton Lavender	Medicinal, decorative
Saponaria officinalis	Soapwort	Medicinal, cleaning
Satureja hortensis	Summer Savory	Culinary, medicinal
Satureja montana	Winter Savory	Culinary, decorative
Scutellaria lateriflora	Virginia Skullcap	Medicinal

Scientific Name	Common Name	Uses
Silybum marianum	Milk Thistle	Culinary, medicinal
Solidago virgaurea	Goldenrod	Medicinal
Stachys officinalis	Betony	Medicinal
Stellaria media	Chickweed	Medicinal, culinary
Symphytum officinale	Comfrey	Medicinal
Tanacetum balsamita	Costmary	Medicinal, culinary
Tanacetum parthenium	Feverfew	Medicinal
Tanacetum vulgare (Chrysanthemum vulgare)	Tansy	Culinary, medicinal, insecticide
Taraxacum officinale	Dandelion	Culinary, medicinal
Teucrium chamaedrys	Wall Germander	Medicinal
Teucrium scorodonia	Wood Sage	Culinary, medicinal
Thymus vulgaris	Thyme	Culinary, medicinal, cosmetic
Tilia cordata	Lime	Medicinal decorative
Trigonella foenum-graecum	Fenugreek	Culinary, medicinal
Tropaeolum majus	Nasturtium	Culinary, cosmetic, medicinal, decorative
Tussilago farfara	Coltsfoot	Medicinal, culinary
Urtica dioica	Stinging Nettle	Medicinal, culinary, cosmetic, clothing
Valeriana officinalis	Valerian	Medicinal
Verbascum thapsus	Great Mullein	Medicinal
Verbena officinalis	Vervain	Medicinal
Viola tricolor	Heartsease	Culinary, medicinal, decorative
Viola odorata	Violet	Medicinal, culinary, cosmetic, decorative

INDEX

BIBLIOGRAPHY

Brown, Deni, *Encyclopedia of Herbs*, (Dorling Kindersley, 2002)

Bremness, Lesley, *Herbs*, (Dorling Kindersley, 1994)

Bremness, Lesley, *Pocket Encyclopedia: Herbs*
(Dorling Kindersley, 1990)

Buczacki, Stefan, *Best Kitchen Herbs*, (Hamlyn, 2000)

Davidson, Alan, *The Oxford Companion to Food*
(Oxford University Press, 2006)

Foley, Caroline, Nice, Jill and Webb, Marcus A.
New Herb Bible, (David and Charles, 2002)

Hemphill, Rosemary, *The Penguin Book of Herbs and Spices*,
(Penguin Books, 1982)

Mabey, David and Rose, *Jams, Pickles and Chutneys*,
(Penguin Books, 1983)

McVicar, Jekka, *Jekka's Complete Herb Book*, (Kyle Cathie, 1997)

McVicar, Jekka, *Jekka's Cottage Garden Herbs*, (Kyle Cathie, 1995)

Phillips, Roger and Foy, Nicky, *Herbs*, (Pan Books Ltd, 1992)

Robertson, Bruce, *Herb Growing*, (Chapmans, 1990)

Stobart, Tom, *Herbs, Spices and Flavourings* (Grub Street, 1998)

Tabor, Roger, *All About Herbs*, (Frances Lincoln, 2002)

Zabar, Abbie, *The Potted Herb*, Stewart, Tabor & Chang, 2003)

PICTURE CREDITS

The publisher would like to thank the following photographers and picture agencies for their kind permission to reproduce their images in this book:

Harry Chambers: 1,2, 3, 4, 3, 12t&b, 13, 14t&b, 15, 16, 17, 18, 20, 21t&b, 22, 23t&b, 24, 25, 27, 28, 29r&l, 30-31, 32, 33, 36-37, 42-43, 44-45, 48-49, 50, 51, 52, 53, 54-55, 57,60-61 64, 65, 66, 67, 72-73, 74, 75, 76-77, 79, 83, 84, 85, 90-91, 94-95, 112-113, 124, 126-127, 130-131 back cover, 133, 134, 135, 140, 141, 142-143, 145, 150, 151, 152-153, 154, 155 front cover main image, 162, 163, 166-167, 168-169, 170, 171, 172-173, 175, 176-177, 178-179, 180-181, 183, 188, 191, 192-193, 194-195, 197, 198-199, 200-201, 202-203, 204, 206-207, 208, 209, 210, 212-213, 217, 218, 219, 220-221, 222-223, 225, 226-227, 228-229, 239, 240-241, 244-245

Oxford Scientific Films:

Pernilla Bergdahl 238; Bill Boch 138-139; Botanica 86-87; Rex Butcher 82; Brian Carter 108-109; David Cavagnaro 88, 89; Jennifer Cheung 104-105; Gulin Darrell 102; Day, Richard 110 back cover; Paulo De Oliveira 196; Professor Jack Dermid 114-115; Dinodia Photo 160-161; Ron Evans 232-233; David Fox 59, 132; Rosalie Frost 125; Christopher Gallagher 97; Bob Gibbons 92-3, 96, 68-69; John Glover 35; Mark Hamblin 186-187; Sunniva Harte 41, 189, 224; Donald Higgs 214; IFA-Bilderteam GMBH 70-71, 98 front cover, 234; Kelly Kalhoefer 190; Ward Kennan 106-107; Geoff Kidd/OSF 10, 116; Tom Leach 123; Gordon Maclean 40, 47, 117 136-7; P L Martin 111; Colin Milkins 78; Steven Needham Mark 99 front cover; John Neubauer 158-159; Richard Packwood 235; Photolibrary Group 164-5; Howard Rice 128-129, 148-149 front cover, 242-243 Pomerantz Rich 26; Janet Seaton 146-147; Tim Shepherd 230; J S Sira 46, 182; Slater, Mike 100-101, 119 back cover; Slocum, Perry D. 58; TH FOTO 62-63, 231; TH Poto Werbung 144; Juliette Wade 211, 216; Eberhart Wally 156, 174, 236-237; Rachel Weill 56, 205; W. Wisniewski 34; Kit Young 103

Corbis 19, 38-29, 80-81, 118, 120-121, 122, 184

The publisher would also like to thank all the staff at the National Herb Centre at Warmington, Banbury, for all their assistance and advice during the making of this book.